T0334235

"Higher education is thirsty for qualified individuals who possess the tools needed to be successful in the public relations classroom. This text could help develop and grow the next generation of public relations professors."

—**Alisa Agozzino**, *Ph.D., APR, Ohio Northern University, USA*

"Professor Smudde's book is decidedly the first of its kind. Never before have I seen a book that tackles the subject of instilling excellence in the teaching of Public Relations by training future educators and practicing professionals in the fundamentals of Public Relations pedagogy. This is definitely the book to read for any student of Public Relations who may want to prepare for the teaching of the college level and for any working practitioner who would like to share his or her experience in an organized and thoughtful manner."

—**Dr. Timothy Lent Howard**, *Professor of Public Relations, PRSSA Faculty Advisor, Department of Communication Studies, California State University, Sacramento, USA*

TEACHING PUBLIC RELATIONS

Excellence in public relations (PR) begins with excellence in education in public relations programs. In this book, Dr. Smudde brings together his industry expertise and over 20 years of teaching experience at higher education institutions to present a comprehensive and cohesive primer for PR educators.

Newly updated to reflect five years of developments in the field of public relations since its initial publication in 2019, this revised edition of *Teaching Public Relations* puts in one concise volume salient matters about effective teaching and learning of public relations. It includes curriculum development and course design plus guides and tools for the work PR educators must do. This book remains the first textbook of its kind and systematically synthesizes current principles and practices for effective teaching and learning and applies them to PR education in colleges and universities. This book, however, is not a book of tips for teaching PR, although some are given at times when relevant. Firmly situating public relations education (PRE) in context, the book goes on to outline principles and approaches for teaching and learning in PRE. Other features of the text include example documents that will help in designing assignments, courses, or curricula, and a comprehensive list of publications, organizations, online media, and other sources for further investigation and learning.

This book is a solid starting point for anyone, especially public relations professionals, considering a career as a full-time or part-time professor of PR at a college or university. It is also recommended reading for current teachers and students of PR research.

Peter M. Smudde has had 16 years of industry experience, including an executive-level position and consulting, and 22 years as a professor of public relations. Dr. Smudde holds the rank of professor and for nine years has been the associate executive director of Illinois State University's School of Communication in Normal, Illinois, where he also was the coordinator of the PR program, which has Certification in Education for Public Relations (CEPR) through the Public Relations Society of America (PRSA), and was a faculty adviser for Public Relations Student Society of America (PRSSA) chapters for 14 years.

TEACHING PUBLIC RELATIONS

Principles and Practices for Effective Learning

Revised Edition

Peter M. Smudde

Routledge
Taylor & Francis Group

NEW YORK AND LONDON

Designed cover image: Klaus Vedfelt/Getty

Revised edition published 2025
by Routledge
605 Third Avenue, New York, NY 10158

and by Routledge
2 Park Square, Milton Park, Abingdon, Oxon, OX14 4RN

Routledge is an imprint of the Taylor & Francis Group, an informa business

© 2025 Taylor & Francis

First edition published by Routledge 2020

Library of Congress Cataloging-in-Publication Data
Names: Smudde, Peter M., author.
Title: Teaching public relations / Peter M. Smudde.
Description: Revised edition. | New York, NY : Routledge, [2025] |
    "First published 2020 by Routledge"—Title page verso. | Includes
    bibliographical references and index. | Summary:—Provided by publisher.
Identifiers: LCCN 2024008058 (print) | LCCN 2024008059 (ebook) |
    ISBN 9781032818733 (hardback) | ISBN 9781032805252 (paperback) |
    ISBN 9781003501817 (ebook)
Subjects: LCSH: Public relations—Study and teaching.
Classification: LCC HM1221 .S775 2025 (print) | LCC HM1221
    (ebook) | DDC 659.2071—dc23/eng/20240322
LC record available at https://lccn.loc.gov/2024008058
LC ebook record available at https://lccn.loc.gov/2024008059

ISBN: 978-1-032-81873-3 (hbk)
ISBN: 978-1-032-80525-2 (pbk)
ISBN: 978-1-003-50181-7 (ebk)

DOI: 10.4324/9781003501817

Typeset in Bembo
by Apex CoVantage, LLC

To the numerous students for whom I have had (and shall have) the privilege, as their lead student, to guide them in their learning, help them break into their careers, and enhance the profession and society in all that they are and do.

CONTENTS

ACKNOWLEDGMENTS

Beyond the students, for whom I dedicate this book, I wish to express my genuine appreciation to all my colleagues over the years who have listened to my musings, questions, grumblings, and discoveries about higher education and being a university professor. Their counsel, wisdom, and humor have been so valuable to me in many ways. In particular, certain people have been especially helpful to me and my formation as an educator-scholar: John Baldwin, Christine Clements, Jeff Courtright, Tim Fredstrom, Becky Hayes, Steve Hunt, Ann Knabe, Lisa Kornetsky, Lance Lippert, Larry Long, John Luecke, Julie-Ann McFann, Aimee Miller-Ott, Barb Monfils, Maria Moore, Priscilla Rogers, Martha Saunders, Cheri Simonds, John Stone, Richard Telfer, Wilfred Tremblay, Greg Velde, Sally Vogl-Bauer, and Bill Weiss.

Of the many professors who have led classes in which I was enrolled, particular ones have had a great influence on me because of what I learned about teaching by being one of their students, and they are: Ellen Barton, Sandy Berkowitz, Bernie Brock, Ron Fortune, Doug Hesse, Jim Kalmbach, Jack Kay, Larry Miller, Russ Rutter, Matt Seeger, Roger Tarr, and George Zigelmueller.

Many students of mine over the years have been wonderfully inspirational. Certain ones, especially after their graduation, have been thoughtfully helpful to me, and I deeply appreciate them: Jennifer Detweiler, Audie Lauf, Kaitie Ries, Ali Seys Preston, and Jill Underhill.

I also want to recognize the Public Relations Society of America's Educators Academy for its fine group of top-notch educator-scholars, with whom I have had the privilege to work and who are always working hard and achieving great results for the profession through higher education. Through outstanding professional-development programs for instructors of all ranks and engagement with the Public Relations Student Society of America, the Educators

Academy provides instructors with superb resources for self-improvement as educator-scholars. Within the Educators Academy there are people for whom I am especially grateful for their guidance over the years: Alisa Agozzino, Barb DeSanto, Marcia DiStaso, Sandra Duhé, Kirk Hazlett, Julie Henderson, Tim Howard, Steve Iseman, Terri Johnson, Dean Kruckeberg, Tina McCorkindale, Shelly Najor, Bonnie Dostal Neff, Bob "Pritch" Pritchard, Gemma Puglisi, Dave Remund, Bey-Ling Sha, Deborah Silverman, Joe Trahan, Sean Williams, and Deborah Worley.

I also am deeply grateful to Jan Murphy and Becky Hayes for their helpful reviews of and feedback about selected chapters of this book that guided me in making those chapters better than what had I originally written.

At Routledge, I cannot express my gratitude enough for the confidence, guidance, and support from Emma Morley, Sophia Levine, Rupert Spurrier, and Kristy Hardwick for this edition and Meredith Norwich, Mary Del Plato, Matthew Rascombe, Angela Graven, Emma Harder, and Sundaramoorthy Balasubramani. Publishing a book truly takes a team, and they all have been great.

Finally and most especially, I am and always will be deeply grateful and indebted to my wife, Patty, and my sons, Matthew and Jeffrey, for their consistent and steadfast love and support on this project and all of my work.

INTRODUCTION

Excellence in public relations begins with excellence in education in public relations programs offered in colleges and universities. This book presents a concise, cohesive, and concrete orientation to effective teaching and learning in PR programs in higher education. In this way, *Teaching Public Relations: Principles and Practices for Effective Learning* is a *primer*, a holistic treatment of the work involved in becoming, being, and succeeding as a higher-education teacher of public relations. This book is not a collection of "tips" for teaching PR (for tips see journal articles about teaching content about PR and Neff and Johnson [2015]). In fact, this book is one I wish existed when I made my career move in 2002 from industry to academia to become a full-time professor of public relations. Most important for readers, because I have been in academia for years after my move from industry, this book presents information, insights, and ideas of my own and from others that should serve well to orient someone when considering to make or actually making a similar move to academia from industry. Also, students in doctoral programs can apply the content of this book for breaking into their academic careers teaching public relations in higher education.

The Need for This Book

With demand rising for competent public relations professionals, PR programs nationally must better prepare people for teaching the subject for effective student learning. In fact, the U.S. Bureau of Labor Statistics (2023) estimates a growth rate of 6% for public relations specialists (principally graduates of PR programs) over the next 10 years, which is "faster than average". Concurrently, enrollment in PR programs nationally is strong, and more higher-ed institutions are adding PR programs to their curricula. Graduate and post-graduate programs in PR (or

DOI: 10.4324/9781003501817-1

almost any discipline except for education) very rarely (if ever) offer (much less require) classes in the teaching of public relations courses. To fill the increasing demand for classes led by competent professors (part-time and full-time), a text (and accompanying course) is needed that competently, concretely, and concisely presents state-of-the-discipline principles on teaching and learning with sound counsel about applying those principles through effective educational practices. Indeed, *Teaching Public Relations* (the first edition and this revised edition) is the first textbook published that systematically synthesizes into one volume insights about becoming a PR professor plus pertinent principles *and* practices for effective teaching and learning for public relations education in colleges and universities. This book's primary purpose, then, is to be a solid starting point for anyone, especially public relations professionals, wanting to begin a career as a full-time or part-time professor of public relations at a college or university.

Teaching Public Relations fills a gap in the literature about the teaching of public relations—no single textbook exists that systematically synthesizes pertinent and current principles and practices for effective teaching and learning in public relations, yielding competent and confident PR educators. I believe the only other book on the teaching of PR (Neff & Johnson, 2015) is a massive 616-page collection of essays (many are research based and all present personal experiences and counsel) that, individually, focus on specific topics for PR professionals (and students graduating with doctoral degrees) who want to become PR teachers and, collectively, functions as a handbook or reference book rather than a focused textbook on effective ways and means for teaching PR courses. Otherwise, there is ample scholarship about individual dimensions of and focused analyses about public relations education in journals and certain reports from PR-industry organizations, which are included in Chapters 4 and 6. So, for would-be and current PR educators, this book puts in one concise volume salient matters about being a professor of PR, effective teaching and learning of public relations, curriculum development and course design, and guides and tools for the work PR educators must do in colleges and universities. In other words, this book reveals what someone is getting into by joining academia to be a professor of public relations.

These salient matters are, indeed, the very things I needed to know as I started my new career as an educator of public relations at a university. There was, however, no one source for me to use to get me started on the path to becoming a new professor of public relations. Having been a student through my bachelor's, master's, and doctoral programs only revealed one side of education, and I needed to know about the other side of being faculty. I needed and wanted to learn about my new industry of academia, and I started with exploring the dynamics of teaching *and* learning. This starting point was pivotal because it revealed how much I had to come to know and master to be an effective educator. Still, a book like this one (had it existed) would have been enormously helpful to get me oriented to my new career in higher education. Through much independent reading, structured seminars and workshops, thoughtful conversations with colleagues and mentors, and frequent application (often featuring trial and error) I developed knowledge, skills, abilities, and experiences that have served me well and continue to serve me well as a teacher and scholar. So, this book is meant to be a solid starting point, not a be-all, end-all treatment. And the research basis for the chapters and appendices serves as the grounding of this book's content and, especially, as the next places you can go for further exploration.

Becoming part of academia also required me to learn about how the industry works and, in particular, the institutions where I worked. There are processes, policies, and procedures that are essential to know and follow in higher-education institutions. Curricula and individual courses cannot be made without due diligence and proper designs and approvals. So too with class scheduling, personnel (hiring, development, promotion, and firing), operations and facilities planning, finance and budgeting, community relations on and off campus, and other matters. Politics in colleges and universities exists as with any organization, and it can be understood and harnessed for the good, the bad, and the ugly that they effect for better and for worse (mostly the former). In fact, the industry of academia fuses the values, pursuits, and fruits of education with the discipline, foresight, and results of business in unique ways that are not at odds, as so many people think, but are truly complementary in providing institutions that are the pistons in the engine of our nation's (and the world's) economy—colleges and universities are the places where the sparks and fuel of ideas mixes with the air of reality to generate the power of knowledge and innovation.

Audiences Addressed

Teaching Public Relations is meant for three interrelated audiences. The *primary audience* is PR professionals (297,100 in the US [USBLS, 2023]), especially those at points in their careers who want to teach PR. The *secondary audience* would be professors of PR programs who lead courses in public relations education (PRE) and would like to improve their own teaching, and this audience would include professors assigned to teach in or design PR curricula when their original field is not PR. A *tertiary audience* (related largely to the secondary audience) would be students of classes on PR research that can/ should address PRE or classes focused on PRE or communication education, especially if these students are undergraduate teaching assistants (UTAs) or graduate teaching assistants (GTAs). Those students may well have an interest in pursuing a full-time career as an academic. In terms of existing curricula in public relations, this book would be core to a graduate class in PR education or a graduate class in research about PR, where the teaching of the concepts and the subject area are directly complementary. To meet these audiences' needs, Table 1 presents features and the benefits of this book.

TABLE 1 Features and benefits of this book

Feature	Benefit
Favors industry professionals and academics alike.	The passion to teach runs deep among those who want to "give back" to others in the PR field.
Structures the complex subject of PR education (PRE) along three intuitive parts.	Presents PRE from the macro level of education to the micro level of student performance.
Presents content in a logical way, from the macro to the micro levels and vice versa.	Chapters flow logically that matter for teaching and learning as a profession and as a student.
Applies current scholarship in teaching and learning generally.	Highly relevant and proven principles and practices in education that matter in PR programs are selected, explained, and applied.
Applies current scholarship in teaching and learning within PRE.	Pertinent and insightful approaches to PRE that have been published are used to link the broader pedagogical principles and practices to PRE.
Provides supporting material for course-management guidance.	Offers selected starting points for planning and running individual classes as well as designing or redesigning a PR curriculum/program.
Presents additional resources about teaching and learning and about engaging in scholarship.	A go-to source for further personal and professional development.
Includes updated content in all chapters, including topics in the areas of advancing technology, diversity, and pedagogy.	Provides readers with newer insights and information since the first edition that will enable readers to perform better as PR educators.
Includes two new appendices, one focused on the tenure track and the other focused on program assessment.	Gives readers with templates for their personal progress as a college/university educator and measuring program's strength against broad expectations for PR education programs.

Because the breadth and depth of coverage about academia plus the literature about principles and practices of teaching and learning are so large, *Teaching Public Relations* necessarily, purposefully, and concisely is meant to be an *orientation* to and a *primer* about academia and starting a career in it. In this way, it focuses on topics that pertain to professors who want to become academics in colleges' and universities' public relations programs. Even on this reduced scale, the material in the following chapters is selected and developed so that would-be and new professors can begin their work as teachers well and then, on their own, build upon the knowledge, skills, abilities, and experiences to become ever better. This book applies research in every chapter so that what is presented is grounded in "reality," and this research foundation should prove useful in this very personal effort of self-improvement. By design, each chapter's references also are meant as additional resources that readers can and should use, if they wish to explore a topic in more depth, and Appendix D can be used in the same way. The close of each chapter includes a point of reflection on the content presented, including personal reflections of my own that I have come to learn over the years and may be shared by many of my peers and others new to higher education.

This Book's Content

Teaching Public Relations presents content divided in three parts, with three chapters in each part (a kind of trilogy of trilogies) how someone may become a PR educator. The first part of the book covers key professional matters for people who want to become teachers, and those chapters are about education as a calling, professionals becoming professors, and professors engaging in the profession. The second part puts public relations education (PRE) in context. This second part of the book covers key matters about the what, how, and why of public relations curricula in higher education, and the chapters cover the past, present, and future of PRE programs and PR students. This part also presents pertinent principles for teaching and learning that befit PRE, covering salient general/macrolevel dimensions of effective education in chapters about general points of teaching and learning in higher education, outcomes for graduates of PRE programs, and the predominant teaching and learning environment for PRE. In this and other parts of the book, some material is drawn from my earlier work (Smudde, 2010), which has served me well in my teaching and my students' learning. The book's third and final part presents approaches for teaching and learning befitting PRE. This section extends much of the material from preceding chapters to present very specific ways of being a teacher and teaching well for student learning about PR. The chapters in this part focus on knowing and being yourself, developing curriculum, designing courses, and assessing learning.

Teaching Public Relations also includes five appendices. The first appendix presents a tool of my own design to help a new PR professor keep track of their progress toward promotion and tenure. The second appendix contains sample course-management documents that can help in designing assignments, courses, or curricula. Examples include a syllabus, assessment manual, and assignment for a real PR course. The third Appendix B presents ideas for curricular and extracurricular teaching and learning for PR students. The fourth appendix presents helpful resources that can be used to further investigate topics central to being a professor. The fifth and final appendix presents a template for an assessment plan I designed the PR program I coordinated at my university. Additionally, a companion website offers material (e.g., electronic versions of the appendices and selected material) that gives other starting points to how professors may conduct their classes.

One final point: Strictly speaking, because *Teaching Public Relations* begins with an introduction and moves into the core content in nine chapters that are organized in three parts, this book could have a conclusion, but it does not. Actually it will. *The conclusion is up to you.* It is what you decide to do, why you do it the way you do, when in your life you make it happen, how you go about making the move, where you decide to enter academia at an institution that fits you, and whether this move is at least mostly what you truly wanted all along. Only you can make the next steps, probably with the help of many people important in your life. My hope is that this book will be helpful to you in some way. Every flame begins with a spark, and you already provided the spark for your flame of being willing to become a professor of public relations in higher education. My wish for you is that, through this book, the catalyst that feeds your flame keeps burning brightly for a long time to come and you achieve much success.

About the Author

I earned my PhD in communication and rhetoric theory (with a cognate in linguistics) from Wayne State University in Detroit in 2000 while working full time in industry as a communication professional, especially in public relations. (By the way, my last name is pronounced smoo-dee.) During my academic career I have made research contributions to the public relations field, focusing predominantly on strategic planning and management for public relations, message design for organizational communication (principally PR), and public relations education. I have published eight books and numerous journal articles, book chapters, conference papers, and other content on vital topics in the field of public relations. My textbook, *Managing Public Relations*, won the National Communication Association's PR Division's 2015 *PRIDE Award for Contribution to Public Relations Education*. Since transitioning to academe full time in 2002 after 16 years in industry, I have actively advanced my own understanding of teaching and learning in all respects, from individuals to entire academic programs and institutions. I am Accredited in Public Relations (APR) through the Public Relations Society of America (PRSA), and this credential is highly regarded within the PR industry and is especially valuable as an educator with a terminal degree and industry experience. In this vein, I was involved with and later a member of the Universal Accreditation Board, including the development of content for its examinations for the APR credential and for the Certification in Principles of Public Relations.

I have worked on school/department, college, and university curriculum committees; led or participated in the development of strategic plans at the department, college, and university levels; and I have served on the academic senates of the two universities where I worked as a full-time professor. I also have been involved at the national level with the PRSA Educators Academy, where I held a board position, worked on its strategic plan, and participated in programming about the teaching of public relations. I also have been involved in the redesign of the PRSA/Universal Accreditation Board's examination for the Certificate in the Principles of Public Relations, which is a credential that

PR graduates who also are members of the Public Relations Student Society of America (PRSSA) may apply for and earn. I have designed multiple courses in public relations (including a graduate class in teaching PR) that have been highly successful. From 2010 through 2023, I had been the PR program coordinator at Illinois State University's School of Communication, where I led the redesign of the PR curriculum that was implemented in the university's 2012 catalog. Additionally, I led the effort in 2013 to successfully obtain Certification in Education for Public Relations (CEPR) for the university's PR program through the PRSA and led its recertification in 2019. Also, as program coordinator, I developed the assessment plan for the PR program and worked with the PR faculty to refine and implement it. In 2015 I led the work for the university-required program review for the PR major. In 2022 I designed a new major program in sports communication for ISU's school of Communication, and if the program is approved by the state, it should be available for enrollment in the fall of 2025 or 2026.

This book, then, takes advantage of my depth and breadth of academic experiences in PR and PR education to yield an important and usable product that is grounded in the wide spectrum of knowledge and matters that are vital to effective public relations education and to public relations educators. I sincerely believe this book will be helpful to you. Thank you for reading it!

References

Neff, B. D., & Johnson, T. L. (Eds.) (2015). *Learning to teach: What you need to know to develop a successful career as a public relations educator* (4th ed.). New York, NY: Public Relations Society of America.

Smudde, P. M. (2010). The education of citizen critics: The consubstantiality of Burke's philosophy and constructivist pedagogy. In P. M. Smudde (Ed.), *Humanistic critique of education: Teaching and learning as symbolic action* (pp. 92–114). West Lafayette, IN: Parlor Press.

U.S. Department of Labor, Bureau of Labor Statistics (USBLS) (2023). Retrieved from https://www.bls.gov/ooh/media-and-communication/public-relations-specialists.htm

PART I
Becoming a PR Educator

This first part of the book covers key professional matters for people who want to become educators and scholars in a college or university. Its principal focus is to give people, especially public relations professionals who want to become educators, information and insights about how to break into the profession, what the expectations are, and how to perform well in it.

DOI: 10.4324/9781003501817-2

1

EDUCATION AS A CALLING

> This chapter addresses the kind of internal/interior inspiration, concerns, attitudes, and issues in becoming a full- or part-time educator in a college or university. It also presents topics that will be relevant in other chapters, especially the next ones in this first part of the book.

Live to work; work to live. Do what you love; love what you do. These two maxims intertwine and reveal the essence of the concept of *vocation*. This concept of vocation is about much more than what one does for one's self. Vocation is an interior calling to which one responds enthusiastically and authentically to muster their strengths, talents, energies, knowledge, skills, abilities, experiences, and so on to engage creatively and competently in service and leadership with and for others. A vocation can encompass one or more jobs one holds in a career, but a vocation truly is more than any job. A vocation is a "calling"—"a transcendent summons, experienced as originating beyond the self, to approach a particular life role in a manner oriented toward demonstrating or deriving a sense of purpose or meaningfulness and that holds other-oriented values and goals as primary sources of motivation" (Dik & Duffy, 2012, p. 11). Teaching is just such a vocation, and in higher education, it combines with research and service. It "is a calling that makes claims on our souls" (Durka, 2002, p. 3).

DOI: 10.4324/9781003501817-3

The Calling to Be an Academic

So, what is the content of this calling to academia, especially to teach? Numerous studies over the past decades have been conducted to explore that topic in terms of personal motivation. In higher education, teaching is one of three key areas of work expected of professors, the other two areas being research/creative work and service. So, while thinking about going into teaching, also think about completing scholarship and service because all three intertwine in higher education. Fray and Gore (2018), in their analysis of 10 years of empirical studies about why people around the world go into teaching, found two broad approaches to understanding people's motivations for becoming teachers: traditional and contemporary. Interestingly, the two approaches intersect to an extent. The traditional approach encompasses reasons that are altruistic, intrinsic, and extrinsic. Altruistic reasons for going into teaching include service to others, desire to help and support students, make a difference, contribute to society, and answer a calling to become an educator. Intrinsic reasons, which Fray and Gore (2018) report are "a primary influence on the choice of teaching" (p. 154), include people possessing a passion for teaching, having an interest in the subject matter, having interest and enjoyment in teaching, being suited for the profession, and establishing one's self as an accomplished authority in a given subject. Extrinsic reasons for people choosing teaching for their vocation include two areas: (1) lifestyle choices that allow for much work-family balance, perceived life fit, flexible work hours, and holidays; and (2) working conditions that feature job security, good working environment, reliable or good income, and job opportunities and career prospects. A third area of the extrinsic reasons is teaching as an alternative career to one's primary career choice, and as such, the alternative career of teaching is not necessarily negative but, rather, a positive thing that links to altruistic and intrinsic motivations.

Contemporary approaches to understanding people's motivations for becoming teachers (and engaging in scholarship and service) examine other influences on people's reasons for choosing education as a vocation. Fray and Gore (2018) explain that contemporary studies examine adaptive and maladaptive motives. Here is where we see intersections between contemporary and traditional approaches to understanding motivations for becoming a teacher who also contributes scholarship and service. Adaptive motives "relate to effort, involvement, and commitment, and include teaching ability, shaping the future of [students], enhancing social equity, social status, intrinsic career values, expertise, and making a social contribution" (p. 156). Maladaptive motives "include factors such as teaching as a fall-back career and the negative influence of significant others" (p. 156). The degree to which someone is driven by intrinsic or altruistic motivations can well influence whether that person also operates on adaptive (i.e., positive, favorable) motivations or maladaptive (i.e., negative, unfavorable) motivations for going into teaching. As Fray and

Gore (2018) explain, "enthusiastic" teachers are driven by altruistic and intrinsic motivations to teach well, "conventional" teachers are similar to enthusiastic teachers but rated lowest in professional opportunities, and "pragmatic" teachers are those who are largely driven by intrinsic and extrinsic motivations.

Other contemporary motivations for people going into teaching are humanistic values, professional vocation, and working conditions. Additionally important is the fact that, "[w]hile cultural beliefs can play a critical role in dissuading some from the profession, they may also construct 'favourable [*sic*] conditions in teaching...facilitating a positive image of the teaching profession'" (Fray & Gore, 2018, p. 157). The greater context for people choosing the vocation of teaching, as it would be in any profession, includes multiple influences from various sources about a variety of concerns that matter personally to one's vision of one's career and life. Instrumental in one's decision to choose teaching, supported by Williams and Forgasz (2009), is that person has some crucial personal values that deeply want to fulfill through a career change (Ahn, Dik, & Hornback, 2017). In higher education, such personal values center on giving back to the profession by teaching the next generation of PR professionals, exploring a field more deeply, and contributing knowledge to it, plus serving the institution, the field, and the community in roles that benefit from one's expertise.

Becoming a Professor

In higher education (generally) as a vocation or "life purpose," focused studies about why people choose to become professors are practically nonexistent. Remember, too, that being a teacher in higher education (chiefly when full time) includes being a researcher in one's field of specialty and someone giving service to the institution, discipline, and community. Doing a simple online search for the topic using various phrases such as "why be a professor" and "professor as vocation" yields many online articles by individuals in the profession, and those articles are on publications' websites and blogs of various kinds (e.g., *Chronicle of Higher Education*, *Inside Higher Education*, and *The Princeton Review*) but nearly nothing from scholarly sources. Perhaps most revealing is the fact that the online articles about being a professor contain advice from authors' personal experiences. In this way, content about why people chose to become a professor very often echoes the altruistic, intrinsic, and extrinsic reasons for becoming an educator, researcher, and servant, which is useful and inspiring. What is important to keep in mind about these articles, however, is that because they are all individuals' personal reflections, they are not generalizable to the entire population of university and college professors. To the extent that you identify with someone's own explicated experiences about why they became and remains a professor could make a difference to you, but in general terms, there is little to nothing in the way of broad insights about professors' motivations for their vocation in higher education.

Even with this ironic dearth of scholarly insight about the vocation of professor, there is one usable vein of sources: job-search websites. The first such website is the U.S. Bureau of Labor Statistics (USBLS), which gives detailed information about a broad range of topics, from responsibilities and salary to requirements and pros and cons of the professorate. The website LearningPath.org presents much of the USBLS's data and findings in usable ways. Other example websites include *The Princeton Review* and JobMonkey.com, both of which present concise and concrete information (in different ways online) about the substance of being a professor. One vital thing to remember about a career as a professor is that, like any profession, there are pros and cons. The best thing you can do is your own due diligence about the profession and find out what it takes to become and be successful as a professor who excels at teaching, research, and service (see Chapter 2). Talk with people that you know are professors and enjoy it (or not). Read articles and books about the profession for all that it is, especially for teaching and learning in colleges and universities. Most important, investigate what any institution is like where you would like to be on its faculty and find out about its organizational culture, student body, overall institutional performance and reputation, expectations for faculty, and the department culture and reputation in which you would teach.

Depending on the institution in which you seek to become a professor, either full-time or part-time, the requirements for holding the position can vary. For someone planning on being a part-time professor, working "on the side" as an adjunct instructor in addition to a full-time job or in retirement, a master's degree, ample professional experience in the field you teach, and adeptness at teaching would be common requirements. For such a position, someone who has been in the profession for a very long time and been very successful, career experience coupled with accolades earned and, especially, accreditation in public relations or communication may suffice instead of a master's degree. For someone planning on being a full-time professor, this career move very often requires a doctorate in the field (or a doctor of education degree coupled with extensive professional experience), sufficient success publishing and presenting scholarly work, and solid teaching experiences backed up with good teaching evaluations. Job descriptions for full-time and part-time positions will state the minimum requirements and expectations. More information about these and related dimensions to working in higher education will be covered in Chapter 2 and later chapters.

Impetus for and Maintenance of Career Change

Different reasons may be behind someone embarking on a career change, from the catastrophic (e.g., layoff and company failure and closure) to the deeply personal (e.g., values conflict with a boss and desire to break into a whole new endeavor). Any career change should be subject to a thorough risk-benefit analysis because there can be some significant challenges to face and overcome, such as the psychological toll from making the change, shifts or sacrifices to accommodate new commitments, financial alterations (especially if a cut in pay and benefits is involved) because of a job and career change, and the need to establish a new personal network in the new professional arena. In particular to public relations educators, they often feel called to their work in academia because they are committed meaningfully to the public relations field, genuinely want to prepare the next generation of PR professionals, and experience a certain organizational identification (i.e., how one psychologically bonds with an organization based on one's view of one's role plus the organization's values and goals, sense of belonging and attachment, and other factors like benefits of working in the organization) with a college or university so they may bridge research/theory *and* practice (Hocke-Mirzashvili & Hickerson, 2014).

A very useful view of the relationship between a public relations teacher and students is master to apprentices. In fact, the ideal full-time professor of public relations, generally speaking, has long been someone with a terminal degree (i.e., a doctorate in the PR field or a closely related field); many years of industry experience with a good track record of accomplishments, especially in management positions; and participation in the profession in one or more professional associations (Commission on Public Relations Education, 2018; Wright, 2011). Additionally, in more specific terms, PR professors also ought to be ready to lead students in their learning in a field that undergoes rapid change; stay up-to-date on usable technologies; be willing to work well with and share ideas and insights with industry peers and leaders; apply their expertise in public relations for the benefit of their institutions and organizations outside their institutions; conduct original research that contributes knowledge about and for public relations; obtain a professional credential such as being Accredited in Public Relations (APR) through the Public Relations Society of America (PRSA) or Accredited in Business Communication (ABC) through the International Association of Business Communicators (IABC); undertake internships with sponsoring organizations to keep their knowledge, skills, and abilities sharp in the ever-changing PR field; and serve as judges, reviewers, or panelists for competitive presentations of research, programs, or projects in public relations (Plowman et al., 2018, pp. 106–107). In these ways, the integration of being excellent at teaching, research, and service is vital. So, preparing your case for being considered for a position as a full- or part-time faculty member teaching public relations in higher education is the substance of the next chapter.

Personal Factors of the Calling

Making the switch to higher education, especially full time, involves "a calling-infused career change" (Ahn et al., 2017, p. 56). Career changes are evolutionary as someone progresses through a series of jobs (perhaps with multiple employers) and instrumental life changes. Simultaneously, a person forms a self-concept that matures with the effects of diverse and challenging factors that affect one's life and career. In this way, then, career change is "natural and inevitable, rather than a detour" (Ahn et al., 2017, p. 49). At the core of such a career change, when examining one's risk-benefit analysis, are the altruistic and intrinsic rewards, while any extrinsic rewards should be supportive to a great extent (Williams & Forgasz, 2009). The calling to be a teacher "embodies the belief that the improvement of self and of human life are always worth whatever it takes to create a better world for all. Of those who see this as folly, we dare to ask, 'What would it be like to teach without such conviction?' We do what we do because we believe that doing it, even in the most trying of conditions, is better than *not* doing it" (Durka, 2002, p. 9).

Teaching itself "is an ancient and venerable task, but it is always a revolutionary one.... All we can hope for as a result of such teaching [of critical understanding at any level] is a kind of person who will make a difference to the outcome" (Booth, 1988, p. 27). In the profession is a range of teachers, and no one becomes a teacher to be a bad one. Indeed, there is something special about teaching that brings out the best in someone, especially in higher education when teaching is tied tightly to scholarship and service. As Palmer (2007) explains, "Good teachers possess a capacity for connectedness. They are able to weave a complex web of connections among themselves, their subjects, and their students so that students can learn to weave a world for themselves. The methods used by these weavers vary widely.... The connections made by good teachers are held not in their methods but in their hearts—meaning *heart* in its ancient sense, as the place where intellect and emotion and spirit and will converge in the human self" (p. 11).

In teaching, the intertwining of one's self with others and a subject together in the greater context of what is going on in the world evokes the dynamism of mind, body, and spirit of teacher and student together. In this way, all are students. A teacher-scholar in higher education is a life-long learner, as is evidenced by the active integration of research/creative work and service with teaching. The vocation of teaching in higher education is one that enables someone to attain ever greater intellectual, emotional, spiritual, and behavioral advancements in himself or herself first through effective and affective pursuits within and beyond the self precisely because teaching is other-focused. Within the context of higher education, the objective of teaching "is that of increasing the student's motivation and ability to continue learning after leaving college" (Svinicki & McKeachie, 2014, p. 5). A teacher owns their vocation when they are gladdened and energized by its pursuits, and that vocation flows within as a matter of personal identity and nature as a person, being genuinely and authentically compelled to inspire learning and contribute knowledge about and service to a subject with others who want to engage.

A Question for You

Why do you want to become a professor of public relations in a college or university?

For what it is worth, here is my story about why I went into teaching. I remember thinking about becoming a teacher when I was in junior high, after my dad had been helping me with some difficult homework, and I thought the process of teaching and learning as we engaged in it (and as I thought about my teachers) was pretty interesting. But not until I was in graduate school, working on a master's degree in writing, did I consider it seriously. On one important occasion, during a conversation with my peers about our ideal jobs, I said I would like to be a professional student, being paid by some large corporation to go to a university, take classes, earn degrees, share my learning with the company, and get paid a good compensation package for doing so. Realizing that idea would not be possible, I concluded that the best alternative was to become a university professor, where I could study what I want, teach what I know, and publish and serve in the field in which I love. On another pivotal occasion, my master's thesis advisor told me during a conversation that he thought I would do very well as a university professor. He did not know about my prior discussion with my peers, and when I reflected on what he said, why he said it, and how much I truly liked the pursuit and sharing of knowledge, I began to devise a career plan. But that plan did not begin and end with teaching.

Through my graduate studies in writing and technical communication, I learned about the great value that professional experience has in many ways. One way in particular was in teaching in higher-education institutions. That is, I believed that if I were to become a professor who had great credibility with students, I had to achieve three objectives: (1) have a substantial industry career in communication and writing, (2) hold a corporate leadership position for a sufficient time, and (3) earn a doctorate along the way. I thought I would, then, retire from industry and become a professor later in my career. I also taught part time for a year after earning my doctorate. It turned out that I accomplished my objectives by 2000, and two years later, giving up a six-figure salary and benefits, I began my first full-time position as an assistant professor in a department of communication teaching public relations. Looking across my 36-year career now, it is split between industry and academia, and the interplay between practice and theory has been wonderful and fruitful in my classes, research, and service.

References

Ahn, J., Dik, B. J., & Hornback, R. (2017). The experience of career change driven by a sense of calling: An interpretive phenomenological analysis approach. *Journal of Vocational Behavior, 102,* 48–62.

Booth, W. C. (1988). *The vocation of a teacher: Rhetorical occasions 1967–1988.* Chicago, IL: University of Chicago Press.

Commission on Public Relations Education. (2018). *Fast forward: Foundations + future state. Education + practitioners: The 2017 report on undergraduate public relations education.* New York, NY: Author. Retrieved from http://www.commissionpred.org/commission-reports/fast-forward-foundations-future-state-educators-practitioners/

Dik, B. J., & Duffy, R. D. (2012). *Make your job a calling: How the psychology of vocation can change your life at work.* West Conshohocken, PA: Templeton Press.

Durka, G. (2002). *The teacher's calling: A spirituality for those who teach.* New York: Paulist Press.

Fray, L., & Gore, J. (2018). Why people choose teaching: A scoping review of empirical studies, 2017–2016. *Teaching and Teacher Education, 75,* 153–163. doi:10.1016/j.tate.2018.06.009

Hocke-Mirzashvili, T. M., & Hickerson, C. (2014). U.S. public relations educators' identification and perception of the discipline. *Public Relations Review, 40,* 100–106.

Palmer, P. J. (2007). *The courage to teach: Exploring the inner landscape of a teacher's life* (10th anniversary ed.). San Francisco, CA: John Wiley & Sons.

Plowman, K., Brubaker, P., Rennie, K. D., Van Slyke Turk, J., Deats, J. R., & Wright, D. K. (2018). Educator credentials: Evolving expectations. In *Fast forward: Foundations + future state. Education + practitioners: The 2017 report on undergraduate public relations education* (pp. 101–107). New York, NY: Commission on Public Relations Education. Retrieved from http://www.commissionpred.org/commission-reports/fast-forward-foundations-future-state-educators-practitioners/

Svinicki, M. D., & McKeachie, W. J. (2014). *McKeachie's teaching tips: Strategies, research, and theory for college and university teachers* (14th ed.). Belmont, CA: Wadsworth Cengage Learning.

Williams, J., & Forgasz, H. (2009). The motivations of career change students in teacher education. *Asia-Pacific Journal of Teacher Education, 37*(1), 95–108. doi:10.1080/13598660802607673

Wright, D. K. (2011). History and development of public relations education in North America: A critical analysis. *Journal of Communication Management, 15*(3), 236–255.

2
BECOMING A PROFESSOR

This chapter explains the expectations for those who would want to be professors of PR from both an institutional and a student view and how to build the proper credentials and expertise to be a professor. A brief summary of the job search process and what is typically required to be successful in it is presented in this regard.

The point of being a professor is to pursue, contribute, and share knowledge. Very generally, being in the business of creating and sharing knowledge means professors of any kind necessarily are experts in particular subject areas in their fields. Professors exercise that expertise, accordingly, when leading students in their learning, creating scholarship or creative/artistic products to bolster their fields, and serving in one's department, institution, field, and community to make things better for others. "The professorial life is distinguished not only by the latitude it affords and the academic freedom it guarantees, but also by the opportunity it provides to pursue any area of study, regardless of popularity" (Cahn, 2011, p. 6). A long-standing view—and a great misconception in contemporary times—refers to academia as an "ivory tower," which is a metaphor for a lofty, rarefied, and almost sacred place of intellectual pursuits separated from the real-world, every-day matters of society. On the contrary, academia is a tremendous place where *theory and practice* of daily life come to play, with professors leading the way because they have the liberty to study what they want and how they want (i.e., given their institutions' frameworks and scholarly conventions) to add valuable knowledge, teach what they know as effectively they can, and serve others on any scale to make a difference for the better.

DOI: 10.4324/9781003501817-4

Academic Freedom

The objective of pursuing, contributing, and sharing knowledge is the substance of the three pillars for academia: teaching, research, and service. (Chapter 3 will give more detail about these pillars.) Institutionally speaking, the free pursuit of inquiry, also referred to as "academic freedom," constructively embraces both conflict and consensus along these three pillars as faculty engage with peers and practitioners about topics in a subject area. And such engagement does not mean that academic freedom is amorphous. That is, there are standards for individual performance within the professoriate, and those standards vary based on one's own college or university, the field in which they profess, and the formal position they occupy as full-time or part-time faculty. So academic freedom does not mean anything goes. According to the American Association of University Professors (AAUP) (2018), academic freedom concerns three interrelated freedoms of inquiry, teaching, and public sharing of knowledge— all of which intertwine the individual, institution, and society. More precisely, the AAUP (2018, 2002) defines academic freedom operationally:

1. Teachers are entitled to full freedom in research and in the publication of the results, subject to the adequate performance of their other academic duties; but research for pecuniary return should be based upon an understanding with the authorities of the institution.
2. Teachers are entitled to freedom in the classroom in discussing their subject, but they should be careful not to introduce into their teaching controversial matter which has no relation to their subject. Limitations of academic freedom because of religious or other aims of the institution should be clearly stated in writing at the time of the appointment.
3. College and university teachers are citizens, members of a learned profession, and officers of an educational institution. When they speak or write as citizens, they should be free from institutional censorship or discipline, but their special position in the community imposes special obligations. As scholars and educational officers, they should remember that the public may judge their profession and their institution by their utterances. Hence, they should at all times be accurate, should exercise appropriate restraint, should show respect for the opinions of others, and should make every effort to indicate that they are not speaking for the institution.

With this definition, the AAUP includes brief clarifying statements that have been added over the years. To provide something of a simplified and pragmatic summary of the spirit and content of those statements, academic freedom means, within the framework of institutional values and policies, applicable law, scholarly expectations, sound argumentation, consideration of prevailing community or social attitudes, and application of principles of effective teaching and learning, professors may, as matter of their role as academic experts in their fields, broach any topic about which they have reasonable and sufficient credibility so that diverse views about it can be invited genuinely, discussed respectfully, and evaluated responsibly in ways that help others and the community in their understanding and growth.

So the romantic vision of professors truly clashes with the reality. Professors work very hard on topics that matter to people in the same field or subject area. And professors often work long and odd hours of any day, based on their teaching schedules (e.g., classes, grading, student interactions [digital or not], etc.), work commitments (e.g., meetings with committees and others), personal habits, project time lines (especially across time zones worldwide), and other matters (see McCabe & McCabe, 2000; Ziker, 2014). The whole idea of experts holding a position that allows them to investigate, work out, and share knowledge is absolutely essential to advancing and improving real things that really matter in the "real world." For the field of public relations, professors are deeply involved in making sense of what works (and what does not), why, how, with whom, when, where, and whether to try them again—the complete content and context of communication between organizations and their publics from the identification of problems or opportunities and the invention of messages, to designing and distributing discourse to measuring effectiveness. The greatest repository of knowledge about public relations exists in scholarship produced over many decades among professors and (more often in the last couple of decades) professors and professionals working collaboratively. In turn, that knowledge is applied in courses about defined topic areas that are essential for people studying to become public relations professionals. More about the content of educational programs will be presented in later chapters of this book.

Aspects of an Academic Career

For any PR professional who has decided to become a PR professor, the process for that decision likely has been a thorough one (also see Buller, 2010; Henderson & Schwartz, 2015). Given the content of the first chapter and this one, you can see there are many dimensions to consider because the vocation of teaching is significantly different from the vocation of being a practitioner of any rank and station. Indeed, it helps to define the industry-to-academia transition as one that "typically consists of an interprofession step in a protean career wherein the incumbent undertakes an effort at an extrarole adjustment. The industry-to-academia career transition results from the development of a particular values hierarchy within the incumbent, and often results in some level of tension in the receiving institution in the form of values incongruency" (Bandow, Minsky, & Voss, 2007, p. 32). Making a career move from professional to professor is not easy, but that challenge and triumph of change is what makes it worthwhile. It is an opportunity to reengage more deeply and in new, dynamic ways with the public relations field that are not possible outside of academe, especially because of the day-to-day pressure of business. In academia, there is a wonderful synergy among the education of students, contributions to the knowledge base about PR, and serving the field in various roles and capacities.

Much has been written recently about academia in the United States, from histories about institutions to analyses of processes to predictions about its future (e.g., Arum & Roksa, 2011; Bastedo, Altbach, & Gumport, 2016; Becker et al., 2018; Blumenstyk, 2015; Christiansen & Eyring, 2011; Fisher, 2019; Levine & Van Pelt, 2021; Newman, Couturier, & Surry, 2004; Palmer & Zajonc, 2010). What is vital to know about higher education in the U.S. (and other nations) is that it is a social, economic, and cultural good in every respect. Like any industry, academia has its problems and its glories. Any college or university, like any organization, has its strengths and its weaknesses. Overall, the value that higher education adds to society far outweighs the demerits. In fact, the outlook for higher education in the U.S. is generally very good, as data from the U.S. Bureau of Labor Statistics (20) shows in Table 2.1. The median pay is attractive among educators, and the number of professor jobs available suggests a high demand for qualified candidates to be professors. Over the next 10 years, the growth in higher education for professors is predicted to be strong, as "118,000 openings for postsecondary teachers are projected each year" (USBLS, 2023, para. 5). When compared to private industry, generally, the one drawback to a career in academia is the pay; whereas, the pay for professors often is less than that earned by people with similar levels of experience in industry. But as a vocation, being a professor has features and benefits that more than make up for that pay difference.

Faculty come from two principal avenues: (1) from academia, after earning a doctorate in their chosen fields, and (2) from industry, perhaps having earned a master's or doctoral degree in their chosen fields along the way. The first route is considered "traditional," while the second route is considered "nontraditional." Ideally, someone with *both* extensive industry experience and a doctorate (either a doctor of philosophy [PhD] or a doctor of education [EdD]) is the best fit for current and future public relations programs in higher education. In public relations, the nontraditional route has become more and more prized over recent years, as people with both industry wisdom and

TABLE 2.1 Quick facts about postsecondary teaching

2022 Median Pay	$80,840 per year
Number of Jobs: 2022	1,333,900
Job Outlook: 2022–2032	8% (Faster than average)
Employment Change: 2022–2023	108,100

Source: https://www.bls.gov/ooh/education-training-and-library/postsecondary-teachers.htm.

academic smarts are highly credible to students because the nontraditional faculty member has "been there and done that" (Silverman, 2010). It is possible that someone with many years of experience, especially including management positions, plus accreditation in public relations or business communication may be accepted in lieu of a master's degree. In all cases, having had some teaching experience is important. Such experience can be gained by leading educational sessions at work, at conferences, or at community venues, or it can be gained by leading a formal class offered through an educational institution. Having been an organizational leader also may be relevant for teaching because of the need to help others understand matters and be successful with them.

Decision Factors for Joining Academia

Before applying for a position in academia, know that there are four key factors to consider about where and in what capacity someone plans to work as a professor. First, there is *institution type*. A college or university may be public, which means it historically was established and its operations have been partially funded by government money from the state in which it is located. Alternatively, a college or university may be private, which means its operations are funded by its own means. In both cases, public and private higher-ed institutions are nonprofit organizations because any profits are turned back into the institution and not to benefactors. Another type of institution is for-profit, which means it operates more like a private institution but a portion of profits are shared with investors as dividends. Any institution ought to be accredited by a relevant accrediting body to ensure that high standards for academic (i.e., student learning) and institutional excellence (i.e., operational excellence) are upheld (Lubinescu, Ratcliff, & Gaffney, 2001). Such accreditation is very important, as institutions must, by law, show on their websites what accreditations they have secured (from the whole institution to educational units and programs of study), and reports about how well an institution measures up to accreditation standards are available for scrutiny. Those reports include the good, the bad, and the ugly about an institution's performance as a place of higher education.

A second key factor to consider is *institution emphasis*, and there are three fundamental types. In all three types, there are varying levels of emphasis placed on one or more of the "three pillars" of academia of research, teaching, and service. The performance standards that uphold these pillars are central to decisions about retaining and promoting faculty based on their performance. First, an institution may be primarily research-based, which basically means that faculty are expected to be conducting research and publishing their work in peer-reviewed journals and conferences and in substantially important projects like books and major projects or reports. Similarly, creative works may be included as publicly displayed and peer-evaluated pieces. Faculty at research institutions also are expected to secure funding from external organizations for research or creative work they plan to complete. Such grants are extremely competitive, so securing them is highly prized as they bolster a researcher's credibility and, especially, fund the work they want to do. In research-based institutions, teaching is minimal to not existent for full-time faculty, leaving most of the teaching duties to adjunct faculty and graduate students. Examples are Ivy League schools and flagship state universities. Second, an institution may be primarily teaching-based, which basically means that faculty are expected to be great teachers who also stay on top of recent scholarship and trends in their fields so that knowledge can be incorporated in their classes. Research and creative work may be only treated as supplemental to the role of teacher, which also includes a sizeable load of service to the department, institution, and field as additional venues to exercise teaching. Examples include small private schools, especially those that are religiously affiliated and locally anchored. Third, an institution may balance teaching and research expectations so that faculty are expected to be strong educator-scholars (i.e., they are effective teachers *and* researchers) who also engage in service to their departments, institutions, and fields. Examples include my own university and others that use faculty performance as scholars and educators as the primary evidence for decisions about promotion, tenure, and merit pay.

A third key factor to consider for breaking into academia is *institution scope*. Colleges may grant associate degrees that students earn over a minimum of a two-year period. These institutions are traditionally called junior colleges, and they host students from a wide variety of backgrounds and experiences. Other colleges may grant only bachelor's degrees that students would earn within four years or so. Universities are institutions that offer bachelor's degrees plus master's degrees and, perhaps, doctorates. Note that some smaller liberal arts colleges may not offer advanced degrees but are still called universities in their name (e.g., Illinois Wesleyan University). Universities typically will be the most likely institutions to emphasize research that is at least equal in importance to teaching or more important than teaching.

Complementing institution emphasis and scope, colleges and universities are further defined in greater detail by The Carnegie Classification of Institutions of Higher Education. This classification scheme serves as "the leading framework for recognizing and describing institutional diversity in U.S. higher education. The Carnegie Commission on Higher Education developed the classification in 1973 to support its program of research and policy analysis" (The Carnegie Classification, 2024, para. 1). The classifications offer insight about how institutions are grouped by their emphases plus other factors. These groupings or "classifications" can be searched for what institutions make them up as well as for in what classification any given institution fits, including summary information that explains that fit in a classification. This framework, then, can be quite useful in identifying particular institutions that may fit one's career plans in academia.

The fourth key factor to consider is the *kind of appointment*: full- or part-time. (Other appointments are temporary ones, such as visiting professor, and are significantly different, come with unique expectations and stature, and, therefore, are excluded from this discussion.) A full-time appointment, which was mentioned in Chapter 1, is the complete package, where someone must fulfill the expectations for teaching, research, and service according to the standards set by the university and the department in which they work. Depending on the institution, a full-time professor, generally speaking, will be required to teach three or four classes each semester (fall and spring only; summer would be optional). A full-time appointment is anchored in a nine-month contact, and additional earnings may be possible through summer teaching or short programs that an institution may offer in the summer or other times of the year to help faculty improve their teaching or complete research. A part-time appointment is solely focused on teaching. Often referred to as "adjunct" faculty, part-time appointments are granted on an as-needed basis but could be renewed because of exceptional and consistently satisfactory teaching effectiveness. Part-time pay is based on the number of classes someone leads, applying a per-class rate that is standard at the institution.

One important additional dimension for this fourth key factor is that being a professor does not preclude you from consulting and freelancing. In fact, doing such work bolsters your credibility in the field, raises the profile of the institution as one that encourages engagement with the community, could earn income for you and/or the institution (depending on how remuneration is structured), and provides opportunities for educational content or research material or both. Being a full-time professor means that position is primary, and any extracurricular work cannot impinge on your responsibilities and performance as an academic. Such outside employment may need to be reported, and your institution would have a process for doing so. Part-time academic appointments would not require reporting additional employment and, overall, allow for a balance of teaching and professional pursuits so that neither area suffers. Being a full-time consultant or freelancer and a part-time academic could work very well, and being a full-time professor and part-time consultant or freelancer can be quite beneficial too. Personal time management and project management must be outstanding to balance work and life matters.

The Job Search in Academia

With your decisions made about each of the four key factors (and there may be others of your own you addressed), it is time to begin the job application process. Remember that, as you would for any job for which you want to acquire, you are making a case that you should be considered strongly for a job and, eventually, hired. So the bulk of the application process involves you making a portfolio about yourself as someone who is qualified to become an academic.

While there are helpful sources that go into detail about applying for academic jobs (e.g., Boyd, 2018; Formo & Reed, 1999), focusing on nine fundamental steps is sufficient, and the content in these areas is necessarily concise to get you started well and keep this book on track. You may also wish to review the first chapters of *Learning to Teach* (Neff & Johnson, 2015) for additional tactics for breaking into PR education in colleges and universities.

Before going into the ten steps, it is important to recognize that the hiring process in academia is usually conducted in a committee system. That is, under the guidance of the institution's human resources department, a committee of faculty in the department seeking a new faculty member will read and rank all applications submitted for an open position. The committee also will be involved throughout the interviews and recommendation to hire someone. Note that the committee ultimately only *recommends* a candidate be hired, as the hiring decision rests with the department chair together with the approval of the dean of the college in a given university and the university's executive in charge of human resources. With this background and your thoughts about yourself that Chapter 1 inspired, here are the nine steps for the application process.

1. *Account for your professional and personal "assets" suited to academia.*
   Starting with your present resume, update anything that needs updating. Next, create it anew as a "curriculum vitae," or CV. While a résumé is principally (if not completely) a listing of current and previous jobs held and education achieved that is organized in reverse-chronological order, a CV differs from a resume in one vital way: A CV presents details (shown in reverse chronological order in all sections) about your work history plus all teaching, research, and service you completed at any time in your professional career. It also, like a résumé, would include details about any professional certifications and awards you earned. Example CVs are available online, and a useful outline for you to begin developing your CV's content is as follows:

   - Education (show by institution with degree[s] earned, including thesis and dissertation titles with the names of thesis and dissertation committees' members)
   - Licensure secured (examples are the Accredited in Public Relations [APR] from the Public Relations Society of America [PRSA] and Accredited in Business Communication [ABC] from the International Association of Business Communicators [IABC])
   - Scholarship (show your published and presented work, using a conventional source-documentation style, such as that from the American Psychological Association [APA] then divide your work into subcategories of publications, conference papers and presentations, speaking engagements, invited work, and works in progress)

- Teaching experience (show by institution or organization and by job title and date with descriptions of classes you led; keep syllabi for those classes on file)
- Industry experience (use your current résumé's content in this area)
- Service experience (show such work by organization, date, positions held, and contributions made)
- Awards earned (show by organization, award title, date, and reason)

If you have an online profile at LinkedIn.com, Google Scholar, or other sites, make sure they all show the same information about you. Being truthful, up-to-date, and consistent is vital. Any social media accounts also must be supportive of you in every personal and professional respect, so make sure you have an impeccable online presence, if you have one.

2. *Investigate available positions in areas of the world that interest you.*

Using what you learned and decided by working with the four factors for entering academia covered previously, find faculty positions for which you would like to apply. Online access to available faculty jobs is vast, so the likelihood of finding suitable positions is quite good, especially if you are willing to relocate. At least two great and highly prominent places to begin are the websites for *The Chronicle of Higher Education* (https://chroniclevitae.com/) and *Inside Higher Ed* (https://careers.insidehighered.com/), as at least these two websites feature job postings from all over the country and beyond in every field and institution. Individual institutions' websites will also list open faculty positions, and these sites will be key to you, if you have a particular institution in which you would like to work. Other very important websites are those from scholarly organizations for the communication, public relations, and related fields. Three key organizations that show open jobs in public relations are the National Communication Association (https://www.natcom.org/), International Communication Association (https://www.icahdq.org/), and Association for Education in Journalism and Mass Communication (http://www.aejmc.org/). The special interest groups in education for the PRSA and IABC can also prove helpful in finding open faculty positions.

3. *Revise your "asset" accounting results from step one.*

Given all the information you gathered from job postings that interest you, go back to your CV and make any improvements that you think would be beneficial to your case. Also, be sure to make notes about yourself, your experiences, and your contributions to the public relations field that might matter in the subsequent steps in the process. Organize all pertinent files of examples to support your industry and academic positions. The argumentative claim you are making—that you are qualified to be a full-time or part-time faculty member and should be seriously considered—must be supported by solid evidence and clear, compelling reasoning connecting the evidence to your claim that matters to the people doing the hiring.

4. *Write statements about your philosophies of education, research, and diversity.*
Because professors are professional teachers and researchers, they must have
a personal view about those two areas. (There also may be a need to articulate a personal view of service.) The point of having these statements is to
reveal who you are in these areas that matter to being a good professor.
Examples of these statements can be found online, and the vast majority of
them are written as short, detailed narratives of about two single-spaced
pages each that explain someone's perspective about education and about
scholarship. When writing a philosophy of teaching, remember that it also
encompasses learning. (Chapter 7 will cover this topic in more detail.)
Begin writing a draft of your philosophy of teaching and learning by articulating what you presently know, value, do, and expect. This way you have
a good sense of where you are on the matter before you go further. Next,
read as much as you can about teaching and learning in higher education,
and make any notes about things that pertain to you, enlighten you, and
inspire you. Remember to consider both on-campus and online educational venues. You could address particular courses you would especially
like to lead and curriculum considerations in light of industry advances and
trends. Then, revise your draft statement about teaching and learning as
thoroughly as possible while also being concise and realistic.

When writing a philosophy of research, you should explain what topics in public relations that excite you and why. Also, address how you
would conduct research on them through one or more methodologies
(i.e., quantitative, qualitative, critical, mixed method) and why that/those
methodologies are appropriate. Additionally, in your research philosophy,
you should refer to examples of your own work that pertain to what you
like to research and, especially, how you plan to develop any particular line or lines of additional research to build on what you have done.
A very useful additional component of this statement would be a "research
agenda," which presents and briefly describes (perhaps in list form) what
projects you plan to conduct, why, how, and for what ends.

A statement about your commitment to diversity, equity, inclusion,
and belonging (DEIB) has become another important document to submit with your application for a faculty job. These statements are narrative
in form and, in addition to your personal identities and experiences in life
inform your commitment to diversity, describe your values, accomplishments, objectives, and approach to advancing DEIB in higher education
as a teacher and colleague. Reviewing perspectives about diversity, equity,
inclusion, and belonging (especially at institutions where you would like
to work) would be important to helping you write your own clear definitions of these concepts as they relate to teaching, research, and service.
Explain how you developed your objectives, what you learned in your
striving to achieve them, and give evidence of you putting your values

and objectives into practice. At the same time, refrain from excessive self-disclosure and using terminology and concepts improperly. Your finished statement ought to be applicable to any institution to which you apply.

5. *Show proficiency of teaching and syllabus examples.*

If you have led collage classes before, you should have a record of how well you performed as a teacher and what courses or class-like sessions you led. If you have not led classes but have led workshops, seminars, or the like, you may have attendees' feedback about those sessions that reveal how they went. Surveys of students'/attendees' responses to your teaching, whether they were in formal class settings or workshops at conventions, would show people's opinions about (for example) your teaching skill, student learning, instructor affect, and teaching quality. You must explain what the data mean from these surveys, including a summary of how the institution and you use the data to help you improve yourself. General or overall data by institution or venue would be sufficient, and you may choose to give data for each course you led. Syllabi for courses you led and would lead also are important examples of your capabilities as a teacher, as they show how you structure courses and their content and assignments for student learning. You need not have summary statements of any kind with any syllabi, but you may like to have personal notes for them that could help you in an interview.

6. *Write a letter of application.*

Given everything you worked through to this point, you must now present your formal argument about why you are qualified to be a full-time or part-time faculty member and should be seriously considered for a particular position. Useful examples for such application letters are available in books and other sources that can give you inspiration for how to write your letter. Thinking of your letter as a formal argument is the key. You begin with your claim that you are qualified and should be considered and interviewed, and then provide reasoning from your evidence. A simple outline of the content of your letter would be as follows:

- An introduction of yourself as someone interested in and qualified for a given position, emphasizing the one key message that matters most (i.e., your "unique selling proposition") that makes you stand out as a strong candidate. In this regard, for example, someone with an advanced degree and PR industry experience plus some publishing would lean on this blending of industry with academia.
- In separate paragraphs, address your record of competence in teaching, research, and service. Tie examples from your CV to the points you make that support your key message, even restating points that you make about yourself in each of these three areas and your philosophies about them.
- Conclude with a summary of your key messages that support your claim about why you are a strong candidate who should be interviewed.

Mention that you attached all requested material and, if you believe it is relevant, any other material that you believe can help your case. Thank the committee for its time and effort in reviewing your application, and say that you look forward to its reply soon.

Note that your letter need not be any longer than it needs to be. That is, whether it is one page or two or three pages, the argument must be compelling, factual, and well-written from grammar to organization. Refer to required statements or documents as needed that flows naturally in your argument. Make sure that your letter targets specifically the academic job you want, showing how your background and credentials directly fulfill the job description. Follow the conventions for proper business letters, using your own, personal letterhead that presents your name as a brand and is consistently used in your CV and elsewhere.

7. *Secure references.*

As you likely already know, having the support of other people who can vouch for your professional and personal character, credibility, and expertise is essential. Because you are applying for a position in academia, make sure you choose people who have some bearing on or, especially, participation in higher education. The character, credibility, and expertise of your references matter because they know you well and would be supportive of you, understanding that you are seeking a career in academia so they can talk about how valuable and valued you would be in this arena. Your references, then, ought to be able to honestly and sufficiently answer any question a search committee has about you. The higher the profile and credibility of your references in PR, the better. It is best to have established academics among your references more than PR professionals, because the academics are "insiders" to the new industry you want to join and can best link your background to the demands of academia. Most colleges and universities ask for three or four references Many institutions will want letters and, other times, institutions will only want contact information. Either way, the references will be contacted. Make sure you keep your references well informed about to which institutions you apply and whether a letter is required.

8. *Prepare for interviews.*

Getting an interview, of course, is a great sign that your presentation of yourself has been successful and that the search committee wants to learn more about you. Make sure you researched the job, the department, the institution, and the department's faculty well so that you can ask pointed questions that bolster your case about your fit for the position while genuinely being true to yourself. There usually are two interviews: by phone or video and on campus. Committees receive a large number of applications for an open position, and from that lot the committee chooses its top applicants with whom it would like to speak to learn more. An interview conducted by phone or by streaming video, with the latter being the most preferred, is the first step. Committees will have a set of questions it will ask all top applicants that are interviewed. How you present yourself and the visual/audio context in which you are present matters, so make sure you take these into account so that your interview looks and/or sounds great. The phone/video interview would likely last about 30 minutes, including time for your questions of the committee. You should have several questions you would like to have answered, perhaps concerning timing for the decision, promotion and tenure process, start-up funds (i.e., money that may be available for new faculty to acquire specialized equipment, software, etc. to do research and, perhaps, teaching), the makeup of the student body, and living in the community.

The next step is an on-campus interview, which would be scheduled with only the top one or two (or three) applicants based on the committee's review of the video/phone interviews. This stage in the process is the last one before the committee makes is recommendation about whom to hire. On-campus interviews are very structured, beginning in the morning and lasting most of a full day. It is best to arrive the day before the on-campus interview day, noting that the institution would arrange to pay for all expenses related to your interview. The agenda for on-campus interviews could include a teaching demonstration (in a real class relevant to the job or in a separate session to faculty and perhaps students); a presentation about research to department faculty; meetings with the search committee, the department chair, and the college dean; and breakfast at the beginning of the day and/or dinner at the day's end with anyone available on the search committee. During all of these points on the agenda, which can be exhausting but also inspiring, trust yourself for who and what you are and know so that you can genuinely be yourself and demonstrate your fitness with and enthusiasm for the job. If, however, in the process you discover something that makes you uncomfortable, it is up to you to decide how to proceed with the day's agenda, and it may be best to stick it out until the end to make sure your comfort level is true. If, in the end, you believe the fit between you and the institution and the job is wrong, say so to the department chair at some point sooner rather than later so you do not waste any more time for yourself and the committee. If you truly want a particular job, send thank-you notes (handwritten or e-mail) to the committee members or, at least, the department chair, mentioning one or more things that are genuinely attractive to you about the position and how you believe you would add value to the department.

9. *Negotiate your contract.*

This point in the process begins with an oral offer by phone and then follows with a written offer with all the pertinent details. Your response to the oral offer should be truly reflective of your personal hope of actually getting a written offer to work at the institution. If you agreed to an on-campus interview and you think all went well, your genuine enthusiasm for getting an offer ought to be obvious during your phone conversation about it. When you get the written offer letter, scrutinize it carefully for what you believe is fair given all the factors you weighed at the outset about entering academia. Research what is fair about the compensation, performance expectations, and any other dimension as they compare to similar institutions in academia and especially in the part of world in which the institution is located. In this way, negotiating a contract for an academic position is very similar to negotiating any other job, but you must work within the parameters of academia and not industry. The likelihood of much or any wiggle room for the salary is very low, and there may be some matters that can be adjusted provided they are reasonable and you make a solid argument for them that shows the value to the institution. Ultimately, your formal, written response of acceptance or rejection of a job offer will be required.

A Question for You

What do you seek by being a professor of public relations?

For what it is worth, and building upon my reflection at the end of Chapter 1, I knew moving from industry to academia was going to "cost" me a lot. I knew my salary would be reduced by around 40%. I knew I would have to relocate my family. I knew that I had a lot to learn about education and being an educator in a university. After much conversation with my wife and some with my boys, who were four and eight at the time, we devised an approach to how we would handle this move. We discussed what parts of the country in which we would most like to live, and I looked for full-time faculty positions in PR at institutions I thought would fit me the best. Because of my unique blend of industry experience and doctoral degree, I felt the best institutions were those that balanced teaching and research. I did not see myself as a grand researcher but, rather, as someone who can excel at both education and scholarship.

In preparation of my move to academia, I had done part-time teaching in business writing at the University of Michigan's College of Business in its MBA program, and I was a part-time teacher of public relations in Wayne State University's Department of Communication in its graduate-degree program. The surveys of students' responses to my teaching were good, and I had them available in the event I needed to share them. I also took several opportunities to enroll in workshops about teaching and learning at Wayne State, and I acquired and read many sources about teaching and learning in higher education. I also had published a few articles along the way and had created an agenda for future research in public relations. These experiences helped me develop philosophies of teaching and learning and of research—statements that were certainly embryonic but definitive and helpful nonetheless. I also, with the help of my professors and online research, crafted my CV, wrote my application letter, and secured references that would be instrumental in my quest.

As part of my academic job search in 2001, I attended the annual convention of the National Communication Association, and there I purposely sought to meet with the people to whom I had applied for open full-time faculty positions in PR. This approach allowed me to drop in on the very people that already saw or would soon see my application, and I could interview them in a way. One of the several institutions with which I met invited me for an on-campus interview, and from there, I received an offer. The reality of the low salary was a shock but not too much, because I knew it was coming. What more than made up for the drop in compensation was the reality of becoming what I had long wanted to become and having the kind of career and life that my wife and I believed would be most beneficial to all of us.

In the summer of 2002, we moved from Michigan to Wisconsin and began a new life together. I loved the change and the challenge, and my family enjoyed the new opportunities in our new home. It took me a couple of months to realize that I did not have to be at work at 7:30 a.m. and stay until after 5 p.m. every day. The great flexibility to do my work as a teacher, researcher, and servant in my field was wonderful, and over the years, I have come to appreciate more and more all that I have and have become and have to offer others through my work as a professor.

References

American Association of University Professors (2018). *1940 statement of principles on academic freedom and tenure.* Retrieved from https://www.aaup.org/report/1940-statement-principles-academic-freedom-and-tenure

American Association of University Professors (2002). Academic freedom of individual professors and higher education institutions: The current legal landscape. Retrieved from https://www.aaup.org/sites/default/files/files/Academic%20Freedom%20-%20%20Whose%20Right%20(WEBSITE%20COPY)_6-26-02.pdf

Arum, R., & Roksa, J. (2011). *Academically adrift: Limited learning on college campuses.* Chicago, IL: University of Chicago Press.

Bandow, D., Minsky, B. D., & Voss, R. (2007). Reinventing the future: Investigating career transitions from industry to academia. *Journal of Human Resource Education, 1,* 23–37.

Bastedo, M. N., Altbach, P. G., & Gumport, P. J. (2016). *American higher education in the 21st century: Social, political & economic challenges* (4th ed.). Baltimore, MD: Johns Hopkins University Press.

Becker, S. A., Brown, M., Dahlstrom, E., Davis, A., DePaul, K., Diaz, V., & Pomerantz, J. (2018). *NMC Horizon Report: 2018 higher education.* Louisville, CO: EDUCAUSE. Retrieved from https://library.educause.edu/~/media/files/library/2018/8/2018horizonreport.pdf

Blumenstyk, G. (2015). *American higher education in crisis? What everyone needs to know.* New York: Oxford University Press.

Boyd, D. (2018). *So you want to be a professor: How to land your dream job in academia.* Cincinnati, OH: Bosley Publishing.

Buller, J. L. (2010). *The essential college professor: A practical guide to an academic career.* San Francisco, CA: Jossey-Bass.

Cahn, S. M. (2011). *Saints & scamps: Ethics in academia* (25th anniversary ed.). Lanham, MD: Rowman & Littlefield Publishers.

Christiansen, C. M., & Eyrving, H. J. (2011). *The innovative university: Changing the DNA of higher education from the inside out.* San Francisco, CA: Jossey-Bass.

Fisher, K. (2019, February 18). It's a new assault on the university. *The Chronicle of Higher Education.* Retrieved from https://www.chronicle.com/interactives/Trend19-Intrusion-Main?cid=at&utm_source=at&utm_medium=en&cid=at

Formo, D. M., & Reed, C. (1999). *Job search in academe: Strategic rhetorics for faculty job candidates.* Sterling, VA: Stylus.

Henderson, J. K., & Schwartz, D. F. (2015). Practitioner to professor. In B. D. Neff & T. L. Johnson (Eds.), *Learning to teach: What you need to know to develop a successful career as a public relations educator* (4th ed., pp. 539–545). New York, NY: Public Relations Society of America.

Levine, A., & Van Pelt, S. (2021). *The great upheaval: Higher education's past, present, and uncertain future.* Baltimore, MD: Johns Hopkins University Press.

Lubinescu, E. S., Ratcliff, J. L., & Gaffney, M. A. (2001). Two continuums collide: Accreditation and assessment. In J. L. Ratcliss, E. S. Luminescu, & M. A. Gaffney (Eds.), *New directions for higher education: How accreditation influences assessment* (pp. 5–21). San Francisco, CA: Jossey-Bass.

McCabe, L. L., & McCabe, E. R. B. (2000). *How to succeed in academics.* San Diego, CA: Academic Press.

Neff, B. D., & Johnson, T. L. (Eds.) (2015). *Learning to teach: What you need to know to develop a successful career as a public relations educator* (4th ed.). New York, NY: Public Relations Society of America.

Newman, F., Couturier, L., & Scurry, J. (2004). *The future of higher education: Rhetoric, realty, and the risks of the market.* San Francisco, CA: Jossey-Bass.

Palmer, P. J., & Zajonc, A. (2010). *The heart of higher education: Transforming the academy through collegial conversations.* San Francisco, CA: Jossey-Bass.

Silverman, D. (2010). *Help wanted: Public relations professors.* PRsay [Public Relations Society of America]. Retrieved from http://prsay.prsa.org/2010/07/15/help-wanted-public-relations-professors/

The Carnegie Classification of Institutions of Higher Education (2024). About Carnegie Classification. Retrieved from https://carnegieclassifications.acenet.edu/carnegie-classification/

U.S. Department of Labor, Bureau of Labor Statistics (USBLS) (2023). Retrieved from https://www.bls.gov/ooh/education-training-and-library/postsecondary-teachers.htm

Ziker, J. (2014, March 13). The long, lonely job of homo academicus: Focusing the research lens on the professor's own schedule. *The Blue Review.* Retrieved from https://thebluereview.org/faculty-time-allocation/

3
ENGAGEMENT IN THE PROFESSION

This chapter revisits the three pillars of higher education and explains why a PR professor must excel in all of them, especially on the tenure track and, certainly, after obtaining tenure and promotion. The chapter then addresses basic institutional matters about university/college hierarchy and the kind of support and enculturation systems available to new professors.

Academia truly is a very busy arena all year, every year. Because colleges and universities are chiefly in the business of education, and education in the U.S. traditionally has run from late summer to mid-spring, people tend to think that the business of education occurs only during those nine months of the year, with official breaks in classes being held within and between semesters. Like any business, institutions of higher education operate over the full course of a year, and the greatest period of organizational activity concerns teaching and learning during the "academic year," which spans nine months, roughly from September to May when classes are held. All the work that gets done is organized in important and useful ways. Because teaching is highly important in higher-education institutions, the organization of work for leading classes is paramount but so is the infrastructure that enables research/creative work and service. Together with these core-business matters, the other business needs of an institution also are in place to support its strategic requirements.

DOI: 10.4324/9781003501817-5

Organizing the Three Pillars of Academia

The first pillar of academia is teaching. In higher education, courses are designed to suit a program or curriculum, and one or more classes (or "sections") of a given course may be offered and led by an individual instructor per class as needed. Depending on an institution, a standard "load" of classes for any faculty member is four each fall and spring semester. (The common nomenclature to express that teaching load is 4–4.) Institutions may give "reassignments" (also called "releases") from teaching one class each semester so that full-time professors have time for conducting research or producing creative works, and in this case, the teaching load becomes 3–3. Reassignments for one or more additional classes may be granted for someone who holds an administrative assignment in a department or other substantial reason (e.g., editor of a scholarly journal or need to work on a funded grant project). Part-time faculty may be hired for one to four classes (maybe more, depending on need and contract stipulations) per semester, and no reassignments would be offered because part-time faculty are solely focused on leading classes. If an institution has any union representation of faculty, contractual matters about teaching and other work would be stipulated and have to be consulted and followed.

Courses in programs of study (i.e., majors and minors) are shown in a university's catalog, and the numbering system can vary from one institution to another. A university's graduation requirements and other relevant policies that pertain to matriculation through a degree program guide how curricula are structured. (More on this topic will be given in Chapter 8.) A useful way to think about course-numbering systems is how students progress in their building of knowledge and skills. For undergraduate, baccalaureate programs, the first level is foundational courses with content that is essential to a broad field of study and could be designated at the "100" level. Such courses feature rigorous inroads to essential knowledge and skills in a field, surveying what a field has to offer in some ways. The next level of courses adds subject-specific material to challenge and expand students' knowledge, skills, and abilities gained in the 100-level courses. Such next- or mid-level courses could be designated at the "200" level. Beyond these courses are advanced courses that go into the greatest depth for undergraduate students, and these courses could be designated at the "300" level and cover very particular areas of a subject. An example of a sequence of required courses (3 credit hours each) in a public relations major could proceed along this line:

- COM 120 Introduction to Communication Theories
- COM 160 Introduction to Public Relations
- COM 180 Media Writing
- COM 220 Public Relations Writing
- COM 260 Law & Ethics in Communication
- COM 290 Research Methods in Communication

- COM 350 Public Relations Campaigns
- COM 390 Managing Public Relations Departments and Firms
- COM 399 Internship in Public Relations (elective or required)

Other courses could be taken along the way at the students' discretion, and those courses are called "electives." Such electives ought to be at the 200 and 300 levels to count toward graduation, depending on a university's policies for matriculation. Graduate-and post-graduate level courses could be offered at the "400" and "500" levels respectively, depending on whether a university offers courses for master's and doctoral degrees. Generally speaking, though, most universities offer undergraduate courses at the levels of 100–400, with graduate courses offered at 500–600, so there can be variation from one institution's course-numbering system to another. But teaching courses at all levels is just one of the traditional three pillars of academia, and Chapters 5 and 6 will address this topic in more detail. The other two pillars of academia are research/creative work and service.

A full-time, tenure-track professor, given the policies and expectations for scholarly or creative productivity, may pursue traditional research, engage in the development of creative works, or both. This work is the second pillar of academia. Part-time faculty may choose to engage in research/creative work, which, together with the full-time faculty's work, make valuable contributions to the field that should advance it. Research encompasses the full gamut of work that spans imagining a project, planning how to complete the project, implementing the plan with relevant resources, creating a finished product (i.e., manuscript), securing an outlet for the product (going through peer reviews of the work), receiving feedback about the product and whether it is in any shape for publication, revising the work for the outlet (if accepted or allowed to be resubmitted after revisions) or submitting to another outlet (if rejected), then having the product published. Publications include journal articles, book chapters, books, conference papers and presentations, and prominent speaking events. Peer-reviewed or "refereed" publications are considered the best. Excellent guides on conducting scholarly research are those by Boice (1990); Booth, Colomb, and Williams (2008); and Moxley (1992). For creative works, such as documentary films, paintings, sculpture, plays, poetry, novels, screenplays, chorale and music scores, and so on, the process is fairly similar but is primarily governed by the scholar's own creative process and the requirements for producing any particular work in its particular medium. The ultimate end for creative works is public exposition, which ought to include peer-reviews or judging outcomes from among other works of the same type.

The third pillar in academia is service. This pillar actually builds upon the other two because so much is required to maintain a field's value and continuing contributions to society. Simply put, service involves "giving back." Expectations for service generally are higher for full-time faculty and for part-time faculty, and any department will guide all faculty in their service pursuits. Service requirements may be fulfilled at various levels: department, college, university, field, and community. For public relations faculty, department service could include serving on one or more committees (as it could also be similar at the college and university levels), field service could include being an officer in a professional or scholarly organization, and community service could include being a member of a board of education or board of directors of a nonprofit organization. Service opportunities vary widely, and they ought to be ones that most complement a faculty member's personal and professional interests, especially along the lines of the field in which they specialize. For the public relations field, natural service opportunities can be found in local chapters of, for example, the Public Relations Society of America (PRSA), Association for Women in Communication (AWC), and International Association for Business Communicators (IABC). Other service opportunities can be found in the Institute for Public Relations (IPR), which brings together industry professionals and academic scholars, plus scholarly organizations, such as National Communication Association (NCA), International Communication Association, regional U.S. communication associations, and the Association for Education in Journalism and Mass Communication (AEJMC), all of which have public relations divisions.

The big deal about these three pillars is this: A PR professor (and any professor in any field) must excel in all of them that play to their strengths as educator-scholars. Given the discussion in Chapter 2 about the types of higher-ed institutions, emphasis on the pillars can differ from one institution type to another. Being a part-time professor means focusing almost exclusively on the teaching pillar, while being a full-time, tenure-track professor means balancing the requirements for all three pillars well and doing well in all of them to the degree expected by your department and university. Boice (2000) explains very well how new full-time faculty members can thrive while balancing the demands on them to teach well, produce solid research, and serve the institution and the field. (Chapter 5 addresses this topic further.) These three pillars, then, are the grounds for evaluating one's professional performance, particularly for full-time, tenure-track faculty.

Tenure, the Tenure Track, and Promotions

So what is "tenure" and the "tenure track"? A common and inaccurate understanding of tenure is that it is "lifetime employment" at an educational institution. Tenure is more complex and does not include any kind of guaranteed employment. Tenure is very similar to any other organization's policies about continuing employment of people. As the American Association of University Professors (2024) defines it, tenure "is an indefinite appointment that can be terminated only for cause or under circumstances such as financial exigency and program discontinuation" (para. 1). The AAUP further explains the purpose of tenure "is to safeguard academic freedom, which is necessary for all who teach and conduct research in higher education. When faculty members can lose their positions because of their speech or publications research findings, they cannot properly fulfill their core responsibilities to advance and transmit knowledge... [because] [f]ree inquiry, free expression, and open dissent are critical for student learning and the advancement of knowledge" (para. 3, 5).

In higher education, someone is on the "tenure track" when they have been hired as a full-time faculty member at the rank of "assistant professor," and the total time that person is on the tenure track is seven years and is called a "probationary period." *Tenure is not automatic and must be earned and maintained.* Through a meticulous process, tenure may be granted to people who have demonstrated a consistent and solid track record of performance in teaching, research, and service. Collegiality (i.e., being a good person working well with others) also matters, and universities and colleges often have a personnel policy in this regard. What is important to note is that one's track record must be well-established every year over the first five years of the seven-year "probationary" period, because in the event that someone fails to perform well in any of those five years, the appointment may not be renewed and they have an opportunity to secure employment elsewhere. In short, someone must make the case that they are worthy of being awarded tenure and promotion.

Being on the tenure track means that someone's reappointment to continue on the track for another year is contingent on institutional funding *and* their performing as expected toward the time they must apply for tenure and promotion. During those five years that someone is on the "tenure track," they have the title of "assistant professor" and work hard at performing well as a teacher, scholar, and servant to the levels required. Annual performance reviews help someone understand how they are doing and what can be done better to excel at the job. Applying for tenure occurs at the beginning of one's sixth year and typically includes an application for promotion to the next level of professorship—going from assistant professor to associate professor—through a thorough process of reviews of one's body of work as an educator-scholar and, if required, letters of endorsement from tenured peers at other institutions (also called "external evaluators" or "external reviewers") about one's research/creative productivity. That process encompasses most of the sixth year of the probationary period, and it begins with the department's review and then proceeds to the college, the provost, and then the university president. And, if applicable, an additional review may be required by a university's governance board (e.g., board of trustees or board of regents). If someone's application for tenure and promotion is successful, they would begin the next year (i.e., the seventh year) with the new rank and with tenure. If the decision is not favorable (i.e., tenure and promotion are denied), the applicant may be able to work one more year (i.e., the seventh year) while also seeking employment elsewhere. Tenure and promotion go together, and very rarely (if ever) might one be granted without the other (i.e., the latter but not the former).

People can be hired as assistant professors with tenure. This circumstance is possible when an institution hires someone who already was tenured at the rank of associate professor at another institution. By becoming a new faculty member, the person may be able to negotiate to retain tenure but begin at the lower-level title to retain the benefits of tenure while still having to fulfill the requirements for promotion to the next level and, thereby, obtain a salary increase commensurate with that level of promotion. Similarly, someone who held a position as tenured associate professor and is hired by another institution may also choose to go back on the tenure track at the level of assistant professor to obtain a greater salary increase upon becoming tenured associate professor. The important point here is that tenure and rank can be negotiated, if and only if the person hired and the institution agree that, under the rules of the hiring institution and given the person's track record, one or the other or both can and should be retained.

The process for being promoted from associate professor to professor (also referred to as "full professor") is very similar, but if someone is denied the promotion, they remain an associate professor and may reapply for promotion to professor at another time, when their track record is stronger. The differences among the full-time professorial ranks can be understood this way: Assistant professor is an entry-level rank. Being promoted to the rank of associate professor with tenure means someone is an emerging leader among scholars in a field. Being promoted to the rank of professor means someone has become a leading scholar in a field.

Once someone is granted tenure, it stays with the person throughout their career at the institution. (Tenure often is not transferrable to another institution but can be negotiated; rank also may be negotiated.) Just like in any organization, excellent performance in all areas must be upheld according to department and university standards. Just like any organization, violations of performance expectations and personnel policies will be addressed according to established procedures and, if necessary, applicable laws. Simply put, tenured professors and part-time faculty, just like people in other organizations and industries, can be fired with cause. The process for determining cause is rather meticulous and befitting of academia, and a similar process would be expected in nonacademic organizations. Tenured professors and part-time faculty, just like people in other organizations and industries, can choose to leave their institutions any time, ideally at a time that does not compromise a department's course offerings, which would affect students' matriculation.

Institutional Organization and Operations

The organizational structures of higher-ed institutions are excellent examples of bureaucracy. But do not let the negative connotation of that word, "bureaucracy," overrule its utility. The roots of university and college hierarchy can be traced back to ancient Benedictine monasteries in medieval Europe, and what is important to understand is that those monasteries were critical to the revitalization of civilization through and after the Dark Ages. All this recollection is not to say that higher-ed institutions' organizations are out of date and out of touch—hardly the case. The point is that, just like any complex organization, a college or university must be structured in the most effective and efficient way so that all its operations can work together to fulfill its mission and realize its vision. Excellent treatments about the business of higher education have been published in recent years, and particular ones that reveal details about how they operate include volumes by Bastedo (2012); Bastedo, Altbach, and Gumport, (2016); Becker et al. (2018); Kretovics (2011); and Lombardi (2013). No two higher-ed institutions share identical organizational structures. And no organizational structure for any organization is perfect, so continuous improvement is essential to strengthen an institution's performance and value for all stakeholders and other publics.

A college or university has distinct operations, with certain units performing particular functions (Bess & Dee, 2012; Gunsalus, 2006; Lombardi, 2013). Organizationally, a college or university's simplest hierarchical structure can be explained as having two fundamental parts: operations and administration. For operations, the largest area concerns academics, which includes all departments and schools (i.e., schools are units that are larger than most departments but not large enough to be a college made up of multiple departments) offering plans of study in their respective subject areas, and those departments/schools are, in turn, organized into colleges and include a graduate school, if such programs are offered. Other operations areas concern facilities and grounds, property control, admissions and enrollment, financial aid, human resources, registrar, student affairs, housing, and others. Many of these operational areas are similar or related to those of complex nonacademic organizations. Administration, just like corporations, fundamentally includes organizational leaders who must oversee groupings of operational areas so that they all work in harmony with each other and, most important, are in tune with the institution's strategic plan, budget, and other forces, especially accreditation and governmental standards. Essential areas of administration include academic affairs; finance, planning, and institutional research; communication and marketing; government and media relations; alumni relations; development; and others. Individual operating units have administrative levels to oversee their day-to-day operations. Official organizational charts for colleges and universities would reveal the interrelationships among all parts of the institutions and, especially, show how those parts make up the whole. When coupled with formal documentation about an institution's strategic plan and all policies and procedures about governance, personnel, students, accreditation, and other performance matters, including news coverage, faculty of every rank can learn the details thoroughly about their institutions' business as an educational enterprise.

For a PR professional moving from industry to academia can be a jolt to your system, but truly it is not too bad (speaking from my own experience). The kind of discipline, politics, expectations, and so on are significantly different but, somehow, similar and relatable. The similarities and relatability at least exist because of the basic nature of work and how humans organize complex enterprises of any sort, especially for business. Fortunately, higher-ed institutions have support structures in place to help new faculty (Bandow, Minsky, & Voss, 2007). Such structures often can focus on, for example, new-faculty orientation, effective education for both teachers and students, technology systems training, funding for new faculty to do research, embarking on a sound research agenda, and personnel support from benefits and policies to employee assistance programs and financial planning. Other support structures may come in the form of workshops or seminars about the institution's workings, and still others can originate from field-based organizations that have groups focused on higher education, especially for public relations. Departments may offer mentors for new faculty, so those faculty can learn about the organizational culture and build rapport with their peers. The more collegial a department is, the more likely people will work well (and play well) with each other, genuinely caring about and supporting each other's progress and success. With departments and universities employing a diverse workforce of faculty and staff, collegiality does not mean no one ever disagrees and no arguments or dissent arise. Rather, collegiality means people are largely sensible and emotionally competent to behave in appropriate ways that are helpful to the group and supportive of individuals, especially so that the work environment is pleasant, plus the way work gets done is effective, efficient, and fun.

A Question for You

How do you imagine your transition into academia may be?

For myself, I started teaching business writing classes part time in the University of Michigan's MBA program, and later I taught a PR class at Wayne State University (my PhD *alma mater*) in its master's program. These part-time teaching assignments helped me begin learning about higher-ed teaching and learning. I was invited to participate in department activities to the extent that I could, and that was a good way to get to know people. I also met with other faculty to learn about their courses and ones I would lead and other aspects of teaching the material in my assigned classes. I undertook part-time teaching while I was working full time, with the idea that sometime in the future I would move from industry to academia full time.

Although I planned to make my career move into academia in retirement, a convergence of events, chief among them being I earned my doctorate and I was laid off from my job as PR director at a major software company, made my entrée to academia possible sooner rather than later. After sending many applications for PR faculty jobs at various colleges and universities in areas of the country my wife and I preferred, and after some interviews, I landed my first full-time job as assistant professor of public relations at the University of Wisconsin-Whitewater (UWW) and started there in August 2002. UWW university provided me with great guidance and opportunities for growth as an educator-scholar in all three pillars of teaching, research, and service. The culture and business of the institution was good, and I greatly enjoyed working with the people in my department and other areas of the university. Those who were senior faculty in my department were especially important in my learning about and succeeding in academia generally and UWW specifically.

Because I saw myself as a newbie to higher-ed, notwithstanding my many years as a student, I was motivated to learn as much as I could about effective teaching and learning in colleges and universities. In fact, because I once was a student, now I saw myself becoming a teacher and needing to learn about that role in detail. In this way, my initial expectations were that I would focus on the delivery of course material. However, the realization that my work as an educator-scholar encompassed both teaching *and* learning was an eye-opener, and I found the prospect of guiding students in their learning far more interesting and exciting. (Chapters in Part 3 will address this topic.)

As a scholar, I learned how various venues for sharing research work, from publications to conferences. I also learned about the importance of building my network of peers in my field so that I could make friends, obtain advice, develop research projects, and participate in field-based organizations, such as the PRSA's Educators Academy and the NCA's Public Relations Division. In this way, my teaching responsibilities and research interests intersected with each other, plus they intersected with service opportunities that pertained to my field and my institution's performance expectations. Being the faculty adviser for the Public Relations Student Society of America (PRSSA) Chapters for 14 years was another way for me to integrate my teaching and research with service, and I participated in local PRSA Chapters in addition to and because of my PRSSA duties.

Over the years, thanks to the combination of support structures at UWW and, particularly, my present institution, Illinois State University (ISU), I made sound transitions into and solid progress at both institutions. My transition to ISU was easier because it is my *alma mater* and, most important, I had six years of full-time experience in academia already, during which I developed a very strong track record in teaching, research, and service that allowed me to be tenured and promoted at UWW in 2006, which was before the mandatory time I would have applied. When I started at ISU in 2008, I went back on the tenure track for three years (the last three years of my UWW record were "credited" to me so that I did not have to go through a whole new seven-year cycle) and was again an assistant professor. I continued building a stronger track record and was promoted with tenure at ISU in 2011. Four years after that, I was eligible to apply for a promotion to (full) professor and was successful in being awarded that rank in 2016. The interconnections among teaching, research, and service are very natural and beneficial to each other, making someone all the better as an educator, scholar, and citizen.

References

American Association of University Professors. (2024). *Tenure*. Retrieved from https://www.aaup.org/issues/tenure

Bandow, D., Minsky, B. D., & Voss, R. (2007). Reinventing the future: Investigating career transitions from industry to academia. *Journal of Human Resource Education, 1*, 23–37.

Bastedo, M. N. (2012). *The organization of higher education: Managing colleges for a new era.* Baltimore, MD: Johns Hopkins University Press.

Bastedo, M. N., Altbach, P. G., & Gumport, P. J. (2016). *American higher education in the 21st century: Social, political & economic challenges* (4th ed.). Baltimore, MD: Johns Hopkins University Press.

Becker, S. A., Brown, M., Dahlstrom, E., Davis, A., DePaul, K., Diaz, V., & Pomerantz, J. (2018). *NMC Horizon Report: 2018 higher education.* Louisville, CO: EDUCAUSE. Retrieved from https://library.educause.edu/~/media/files/library/2018/8/2018horizonreport.pdf

Bess, J. L., & Dee., J. R. (2012). *Understanding college and university organization: Theories for effective policy and practice* (2 vols.). Sterling, VA: Stylus Publishing.

Boice, R. (1990). *Professors as writers: A self-help guide to productive writing.* Stillwater, OK: New Forums.

Boice, R. (2000). *Advice for new faculty members: Nihil Nimus.* Boston, MA: Pearson.

Booth, W. C., Colomb, G. G., & Williams, J. M. (2008). *The craft of research* (3rd ed.). Chicago, IL: University of Chicago Press.

Gunsalus, C. K. (2006). *The college administrator's survival guide.* Cambridge, MA: Harvard University Press.

Kretovics, M. A. (2011). *Business practices in higher education: A guide for today's administrators.* New York: Routledge.

Lombardi, J. V. (2013). *How universities work.* Baltimore, MD: Johns Hopkins University Press.

Moxley, J. M. (1992). *Publish, don't perish: The scholar's guide to academic writing and publishing.* Westport, CT: Praeger.

PART II

Public Relations Education (PRE) in Context

This second part of the book covers key matters about the what, how, and why of public relations curricula in higher education. It presents a holistic view of public relations education in colleges and universities, a summary of education theories and practices, and selected pedagogical approaches that fit PRE well.

DOI: 10.4324/9781003501817-6

4

AN OVERVIEW OF PUBLIC RELATIONS EDUCATION

This chapter covers the emergence, growth, and direction of public relations education, primarily in the U.S. Particular touchpoints are higher-ed PR programs' development and evolution that coincided with growing industry needs. Especially important are the recommendations for strengthening PR education for undergraduate and graduate programs and what those recommendations portend for the further success of higher-ed PR programs.

Public relations practices, as we conceive of them today, can be identified as far back as ancient civilizations that provided information for people about achieving high crop yields (see Cutlip, 1994, 1997; Cutlip, Center, & Broom, 1994). In U.S. history, the Boston Tea Party can be seen as a publicity stunt, and *The Federalist Papers*, which were instrumental in securing the ratification of the United States Constitution, can be viewed as public relations. Yet the formal profession did not emerge until the end of the nineteenth century, when journalists became the first PR pros because corporations hired them to obtain more favorable stories in the newspapers, which the former journalists knew well from the inside. Public relations also grew out from the labor movements in the early 1900s, primarily within the steel, oil, meat-packing, and railroad industries, and were fertilized by the muckraking journalistic practices about what was going on; thus, both business and government alike adopted aggressive practices of public communication and defense (Cutlip, 1997, p. 23). Again, journalists were early PR professionals in corporations that hired them because they knew the news business and how to get coverage far better than corporate executives and their staffs.

DOI: 10.4324/9781003501817-7

The Origin of Public Relations Education

Formal education in public relations was not formulated and offered until the 1920s. Wright's (2011) valuable account of the development of public relations education in the U.S. and Canada (also see Welch, 2015) shows that the first PR course in higher education was offered at the University of Illinois in 1920 and led by Joseph P. Wright, who was the university's publicity director. Edward L. Bernays led a PR course in 1923 and 1924 at New York University. The first degree program (for a master's degree) in public relations was offered at Boston University in 1947, and the program was part of the university's School of Public Relations, which now is the College of Communication and covers more subjects than just PR. The 1970s featured growth of PR education programs in North America, especially in the U.S. In fact, "most of the early university-based public relations education programs in the USA were based at major, research-oriented universities... [, but] much of this 1970s expansion took place within smaller, regional and mid-major institutions. And although most of the original public relations degree programs in the USA were based in journalism colleges, schools or departments, a good number of these new programs were located in speech-communication departments, many of which would later drop 'speech' from their titles and become known as communication departments" (Wright, 2011, p. 244). The expansion of PR education programs in higher education has continued since the 1980s, with more programs emerging precipitously that offer a fairly common core of courses (i.e., overview of PR, writing, research, campaigns, and internship) with a variety of electives. Today there are 1,273 higher-ed institutions offering baccalaureate degree programs in "communications/public relations" (Commission on Public Relations Education, 2018, p. 96).

Naturally, the earliest PR programs served as models for other U.S. institutions that wanted their own PR programs, which perpetuated a particular orientation about the practice and how to teach it. And the amalgamation of U.S. undergraduate or graduate public relations programs became the standard for such programs in other countries. The key characteristic of the U.S. model long has been offering PR programs in journalism schools, which, although understandable given the history of the field, has proven not to be consistent with the demands of society and business (Wright, 2011). The rapid growth of the field and, in turn, higher-ed academic programs to support the growing PR profession resulted in undergraduate programs that were housed in departments of speech communication and sometimes business, where the majors were treated as "concentrations," "sequences," or "tracks" (depending on an institution's terminology) within an already-existing major, such as communication or marketing. That spread of PR programs in various departments (including departments of mass media, business, social sciences, humanities) remains today and adversely contributes to understanding what public relations is and involves. Ideally, PR educators have long preferred being in their own departments or schools, where they can control their own destinies by managing all the necessary resources and making decisions about curricula accordingly. As things are now, generally, enrollment in existing public relations programs is significant, being strong contributors to departmental matriculation rates and, thereby, tuition, which means PR programs are unlikely to be moved, diminished, or cut (Commission on Public Relations Education, 2012, pp. 95–96).

"Standards" for Public Relations Education

Public relations once relied on deep associations with news organizations and fostered one-way communication, but this situation has been displaced, especially over the last couple of decades, by multiple and converging media that span the globe and feature two-way communication (Wright, 2011). In fact, a consortium of public relations industry groups and scholars assembled in 1973, named the Commission on Public Relations Education (CPRE), saw the dynamics changing in the 1970s. Over the ensuing years the Commission sought the input of industry leaders, educators, hiring managers, and entry-level professionals to produce many crucial and instrumental reports (1975, 2001, 2006, 2012, 2015, 2018, 2020, 2021, 2022, and 2023) about the state and the future of undergraduate public relations education. Additional papers by Tench and Deflagbe (2008), Toth and Aldoory (2010), the Canadian Public Relations Society (2010), and Jain (2017) examined undergraduate PR programs in and beyond North America. Plus, in examinations of graduate curricula in public relations, the Commission on Graduate Study in Public Relations (1985); Aldoory and Toth (2000); Hon, Fitzpatrick, and Hall (2004); Shen and Toth (2008); and the Commission on Public Relations Education (2012) produced insightful analyses and guidance about public relations education at this advanced level.

The CPRE (2023b) also published reports about 2019, 2021, and 2022 "summits" between industry and academia that examined industry demands, trends, and expectations for PR professionals along with academia's demands, curricula, and capabilities for preparing students for PR careers. In addition, CPRE has shared other valuable reports about other vital topics, including new factors in PR education, ethics, online learning, writing, gender equality, among others. The CPRE's (2023a) report, which was prepared in celebration of the 50th anniversary of the CEPR, is especially useful and insightful because of its broad and thorough examination of the public relations field, especially addressing very timely topics at the time of its publishing. Specifically, the report is largely one about the results of new studies that explored the field in depth that applies to both the practice and the education of PR. Educators should consult this report (and the others) at least for their treatment of specific topics that could be worthwhile to present to students—to show how well both industry and academia are in sync about the requirements, demands, and opportunities of public relations.

One important take-away from all these reports is that, over the last few decades, the public relations profession has become especially introspective and rigorous about how people can best become educated and prepared for the demands of the field. Scanning the contents of the reports published over time shows the evolution of public relations education as always responsive to the dynamics of society, industry, and technology, and always applying the ever-building knowledge about these and other arenas of life and their intersections with the profession. The reports present concrete realities of the PR profession and strong prescriptions for making education about PR more potent so that greater value is added to organizations and society through good, competent PR professionals who ethically produce excellent work.

These reports about public relations education serve as portals to the past that show how far the field has come in a fairly short span of time. Checking to see whether and how much any predictions and prescriptions for future PR education (PRE) came to pass from report to report further shows how well curricula have aligned with the changing needs of society, business, and other arenas of life (see Kim & Johnson, 2011; for independent examinations of PRE also see Crooks [2017] and Xie, Schauster, & Neill [2018]). Although an analysis of those predictions and prescriptions across all these reports certainly would be interesting, for our purposes here, the focus is on the most recent assessment for PRE.

That recent outlook comes from the Commission on Public Relations Education (2018), which is the most-recent and the most-thorough treatment about the recommended content for *undergraduate* PR curricula. In its 168 pages, the report's principal content presents detailed data description, analysis, and recommendations from a "summit" of industry leaders and educators *and* an omnibus survey of managers who hire entry-level PR employees and of educators—all to investigate 15 areas material to undergraduate PRE and excellent PR practice that matter now and, particularly, in the future. Those areas are learning objectives, undergraduate curriculum, ethics, theory, research, technology, academic structure and governance, educator credentials, online education, program certification and accreditation, internships, professional and preprofessional organizations, diversity and inclusion, global perspectives on PRE, and future matters for PRE. Table 4.1 presents a composite view of the report's findings-based recommendations organized by each PRE area.

In terms of *graduate* PRE, the Commission on Public Relations Education's (2012) report presents the most-recent specific findings and recommendations for curricula leading to a master's degree in public relations. Again, using input from industry leaders, educators, hiring managers, and PR professionals, the content of this report addresses five dimensions: curriculum, admission standards, program delivery, necessary resources, and global graduate PRE standards. Table 4.2 presents a composite view of the findings-based recommendations in that report.

While these composite views of PRE have great utility in providing a usable and useful framework for creating, maintaining, scrutinizing, and improving PR programs at the undergraduate and graduate levels, these same views (and the reports that address them) are only just suggestions. Even so, as suggestions, these composite views are robust, being based on sound research that gathered the requisite information to advance them at all, which underscores their great value and

TABLE 4.1 Composite view of undergraduate PRE from the Commission on Public Relations Education (2018)

Undergraduate PRE area	Findings-based recommendations
Learning objectives	Among practitioners and educators, multiple knowledge, skills, and abilities (KSAs) were ranked, and the top five in each area are as follows: knowledge (ethics, diversity and inclusion, cultural perspective, business acumen, and social issues), skills (writing, communication, social media management, research and analytics, and editing), and abilities (creative thinking, problem solving, critical thinking, analytical thinking, and strategic planning). Of the KSAs, skills and abilities are most demanded. Learning objectives in PRE courses, then, should foster learning that builds competence in the following: diversity and inclusion, social issues, ethics, social media, research and analytics, communication and storytelling, and all abilities areas.
Undergraduate curriculum	The traditional undergraduate PR curriculum comprises five core courses of introduction to PR, research methods, writing, campaigns (case studies), and internships. Practitioners and educators, recognizing varying resource differences among institutions, recommend that the five-course core should include ethics. Additional subjects could include business literacy, content creation for any medium, data analytics, digital technology, and measurement/evaluation for effectiveness and value added.
Ethics	Ethics issues of truthfulness in any communication and organizational transparency, especially during decision-making, are at the heart of this area. Because competence in ethics is essential to the field, practitioners and educators primarily recommend PRE programs include a course specifically on PR ethics, and they recommend ethics be integrated in all PR courses and include moral philosophy, cases, and simulations.
Theory	The importance of theory is high, as knowledge and application of them prove instrumental in real situations, from the micro level (individual audience members) to the macro level (society as a whole). Practitioners and educators recommend the teaching of the practical importance and utility of theory, the explication of theoretical material for practitioners in their contexts to meet their needs, the connection of principles and practices in organizational contexts, the integration of business and management theories that apply to PR, and the emphasis on the dynamics of change in theory.
Research	Entry-level employees are not sufficiently competent in conducting research and analyzing data. Students must master fundamental research methods and skills, not merely be exposed to them through lecture and secondary sources. Practitioners and educators recommend the topics of The Barcelona Principles for PR research and the nature, purpose, types, methods, and analysis of research be part of PRE curriculum.

(Continued)

TABLE 4.1 (Continued)

Undergraduate PRE area	Findings-based recommendations
Technology	The range of technology available for public relations is vast, and entry-level employees must be sufficiently competent in the range of devices, platforms, and methods available for creating and curating content , including artificial intelligence (AI; see also Vujnovic, Swiatek, Kruckeberg, & Galloway, 2023). Practitioners and educators recommend that students understand quantitative analysis of business data, know how to write for every venue (digital and analog), have experience using technology in courses, learn how technology concepts matter in nontechnology courses, and have instructors who are up-to-date on technology, especially as users.
Academic structure and governance	Inconsistency of where PR programs are housed contributes to confusion about PR as a profession. Practitioners and educators recommend working with practitioners on industry-current content, teaching always under the moniker of "public relations," having unwavering support for the program at the university level, involving alumni and practitioners for financial and other support for PR programs, assembling advisory boards to counsel the program for its curriculum and course updates, establishing partnerships with the on-campus PR office, and collaborating with other relevant academic departments.
Educator credentials	Executives report that the best entry-level employees come from PR programs that have professors who have industry experience and academic credentials—they bridge well theory and practice by who they are and what they have accomplished. Educators and practitioners recommend that PR educators be adept at teaching in a dynamic field of education, stay up to date on technology, collaborate and exchange ideas with those in industry, have ample industry experience, participate in university committees and advocate effective PR, conduct research, become Accredited in Public Relations (APR), hold leadership positions in PR industry organizations, pursue occasional internships for themselves, and serve as judges in competitions or speakers for on-campus events.
Online education	The appeal and growth of online education opportunities cannot be ignored, and PR programs have been making strides in offering online courses and degree programs. Educators and practitioners recommend making financial investments necessary for robust online learning, ensuring online educational experiences are as rigorous as traditional on-site classes, and have and apply effective assessment methods to determine online program quality from learning outcomes to job placement.

Program certification and accreditation	Upholding set standards for educational excellence in the teaching and learning of PR is key to demonstrating the quality, rigor, and value of PR programs in higher ed. Educators and practitioners recommend increased promotions about the importance and value of program certification/accreditation, expanded efforts to recruit and train evaluators of programs seeking certification/accreditation, tailored certification/accreditation for nondegree programs, and expanded roles on the certification/accreditation organizations' boards.
Internships	Hands-on, real-world experiences in PR organizations is considered crucial to learning about the profession and developing skills and abilities in PR. Educators and practitioners recommend all internships be paid; all interns be supervised by PR professionals who actively direct their learning; all internships should be evaluated by both the intern and the supervisor; internship programs should be led by a dedicated coordinator; internships should be required in PR programs; internship courses should be subject to regular assessments for educational quality; everyone involved in internships understand the legal, institutional, and program requirements; interns must have completed all prerequisite courses; and fostering diversity among students enrolling in internships.
Professional and preprofessional organizations	Profession-focused organizations for practitioners and for students are instrumental in helping students to actively make their ways into the PR careers. Educators and practitioners recommend exposure to the practice of PR outside of classes in student-run firms or PR departments/organizations on and off campus, guest speakers from industry in classes or student-run organizations, establishment of and participation in chapters of PRSSA or IABC on campus, and gaining a Certificate in the Principles of Public Relations.

(Continued)

TABLE 4.1 (Continued)

Undergraduate PRE area	Findings-based recommendations
Diversity	Diversity, equity, inclusion, and belonging (DEIB) are central to effective professional, organizational, and social successfulness, and changes in PRE are needed to reap the value of DEIA. The key matter is enabling students from diverse backgrounds to see themselves in the PR profession. (See Kern-Foxworth [2015], Landis [2019], and Tsetsura [2011] for curriculum-specific ideas.) Educators and practitioners recommend focusing on the role of leaders in making DEIB work successfully, securing necessary resources and support to help students from underrepresented groups, recruiting diverse pool of candidates for faculty positions and student enrollment, retaining students and faculty from underrepresented groups, teaching diversity and multicultural perspectives in courses, advocating for DEIB being a true organizational value, and moving quickly and effectively on all DEIB matters.
Global perspectives on PRE	The exchange of ideas, principles, and practices for effective PR spans the globe just as the profession itself spans the globe. Educators and practitioners recommend emphasis on global interconnectedness, active exchange of ideas among PR professionals and educators, increased dialog with institution administration about PR's global significance, creation of international accreditation for PRE programs, focused instruction about global PR, and promotion of international exchange and study-abroad programs.
Future matters for PRE	The biggest challenge is turning the recommendations into reality. The Council on Public Relations Education (CPRE) presents the following action steps: conducting additional research on teaching preparation and professional experience for faculty of all ranks, full- and part-time; creating a framework for helping PRE programs to add a sixth core course on ethics into their curricula; exploring effective online education; defining PR educators' role in fostering diversity in the profession; measuring the progress toward realizing CPRE's recommendations from this and the previous report; improving entry-level employees' writing quality; and continuing industry-educator dialog about all PRE matters.

TABLE 4.2 Composite view of graduate PRE from the Commission on Public Relations Education (2012)

Graduate PRE area	Findings-based recommendations
Curriculum	Graduate programs in PR follow one of two pathways. The first is to lead to a doctorate and, in this case, the recommendations are that such programs offer additional courses on research and require a thesis as the capstone to the degree program. The second leads to industry and, in this case, the recommendations are for courses focused in specialization areas of PR (e.g., healthcare, sports and entertainment, social services) and for internship/practicum/cooperative education.
Admission standards	Students may enter a graduate program with or without a bachelor's degree in PR. In the former case, students are in a better position to advance in their KSAs than those in the latter case who lack exposure to the fundamentals from a PRE program. Those without a PR degree but have had industry experience and accreditation as a communication professional (APR or ABC) can make up for the difference. Completing study of the core courses for PR programs still would be essential. Students should be good people with strong personal character; work ethic; intelligent; positive attitudes toward the field, learning, and scholarship; and genuine respectfulness of others.
Program delivery	Graduate degree programs can be offered as traditional on-campus courses (with or without web-facilitated learning tools), blended/hybrid courses that incorporate both online and face-to-face/on-campus experiences, and online courses that do not have physical face-to-face meetings. Recommendations for program delivery are: adhering to highest standards for effective teaching and learning no matter what mode is used, and students perform due diligence in choosing the mode that works for them; employing the rigor, advanced learning, and fostering of scholarly competence expected of graduate programs; managing expectations about graduate study as well beyond the experiences of baccalaureate programs; setting and upholding high performance standards of students so they contribute well to the field, share knowledge with the next generation, conduct value-added research or creative projects, apply theory and best practices to their work, and serve the profession and society well.

(Continued)

TABLE 4.2 (Continued)

Graduate PRE area	Findings-based recommendations
Necessary resources	Several categories of resources are covered and given recommendations. For faculty, they should hold a doctorate and professional experience, but at minimum they should hold a master's degree and professional experience, depending on a professional's background and credentials. Faculty also should hold an official accreditation credential and actively pursue ongoing professional development as an educator and scholar. For finance and facilities, graduate PR programs should have more autonomy for facilities and budget management, attract external funding for the program and its students, and benefit from support for global initiatives for faculty and students. For marketing support, graduate programs should employ strategically appropriate and effective methods for promoting the program, attracting diverse students and faculty, and asserting the value of a graduate degree in PR. For internships/professional field experiences, programs should promote them to all students, even if it is to encourage students who already hold PR positions to link their professional work with their studies. For technology, ensure current technology is deployed and updated that is comparable to what is used in the field, and all should perform well the work required for advancing in learning and competence in PR, from ideation to measurement/evaluation. For industry-academe interaction, leaders in the profession counsel educators about PRE programs, both help practitioners to become educators, and practitioners and their organizations collaborate on educational or scholarly efforts.
Global graduate PRE standards	Although one standard for graduate education that would apply in all countries is an ideal, the practical matter is that such a standard is elusive because of the culture and various forces at play in any given nation and its educational system. Particular nations' approaches, like those developed in the U.S.A. and Canada, can serve as models for institutions in other nations that they can tailor to their circumstances and requirements. The Global Alliance for Public Relations and Communication Management was established in 2000 to help develop a "world standard for public relations curricula" in higher education.

utility. At the same time, the Commission on Public Relations Education (2018) presents this important reminder: "*The needs of industry are complex and changing, and there's no one-size-fits-all list of knowledge, abilities, and skills that is applicable for every job in every public relations setting.* CPRE's (2023a) report is a especially important and useful in this regard. This is today's reality for students aspiring to a career in public relations, those who seek to educate and prepare them, and those who want to hire them" (p. 25; italics in original).

Future Matters for PRE

The continuing evolution of the field of public relations in industry and academe includes all its principles, practices, tools, and methods. PRE is instrumental in this evolution and the preparation of competent, conscientious, self-aware (attitudes and behaviors), and ethical public relations professionals—these are Good people inspiring cooperation well between organizations and their publics. Thanks to the many decades of hard, expert work and the successfulness of professionals *and* scholars the world over, the image and reputation of public relations as a vital, ethical, and valuable organizational and social function has improved greatly and is being well-established in society (see Coombs & Holladay, 2014; Edwards & Hodges, 2011; L'Etang, 2004/2012; Pieczka & L'Etang, 2001; Taylor, 2010; Yang & Taylor, 2013). Fundamentally, public relations requires a high degree of professionalism among all practitioners at any level, and this professionalism involves doing the right thing in the right way at the right time for the right people for the right reasons.

Successful new and seasoned public relations professionals, who come through higher-ed PR programs, will be those who uphold and are recognized for high degrees of professionalism and ethics that they began to develop in their studies and refined and passed along during their careers. PRE in the future naturally will address matters of changes in society and economy, business and industry, environment, technology, and others. The particulars of what the changes may be already have been addressed in the composite views of undergraduate and graduate PRE. Human nature, however, seems to be consistent enough to point to future directions in PRE. In this way, as Duhé (2016) suggests, PRE will need to guide students in their thinking in the future tense and do so with a strategic bias and business awareness. Duhé further explains that students will also have to value and participate in multidimensional and interdisciplinary thinking and doing that adds value to organizations and society, amass sufficient (or better) abilities in working with data of all kinds to derive meaning, and propose viable actions for the greater good. Advances in and the ethics of the use of artificial intelligence for all manner of content creation is particularly paramount for the PR profession and education. Additionally, as Gallup and Bates College (2019) argue, students will need to find the kind of personal and professional purpose that is deeply fulfilling to them so they thrive in their careers in all these dimensions and beyond, wherever their careers take them.

A Question for You[*]

As you consider becoming a new PR professor, what do you know about public relations education?

For what it is worth, when I became a full-time professor of public relations in the fall semester of 2002, I truly didn't know very much about public relations education. The best I knew was about individual courses I either led, which only intersected with PR because they were classes in a business writing program and one graduate course in PR, or knew about because I knew people enrolled in or leading them. I did not have a holistic, systematic understanding of PRE, and it would have been nice at least to have a high-level view like this book. So, I had to research PR programs and their courses at the universities I sought to join, and in the process I discovered a wide variety of topics along with a fairly stable set of core courses across institutions' PR programs. Because of my independent research about teaching and learning, which I described at the end of Chapter 3, I was able to develop my own knowledge, skills, and abilities for being a PR educator. I also met and got to know many successful PR educators and attended conference sessions that introduced me to resources (published, organizational, and interpersonal) and shared ideas about effective teaching and learning in PR curricula.

One of the most important experiences I had in the formation of my thinking and doing in PRE was connecting the dots among my industry experiences, my philosophy of teaching and learning, and my plans and experiences leading PR classes. The more I learned about education from the perspectives of teaching and of learning, the more I understood how and why things work (or don't) and how and why I can make things better for my students and myself. The micro and macro levels of principles and practices were very intertwined and easy enough to account for appropriately. There were far more trial-and-error approaches in my teaching at the beginning, but it was tempered by the guidance of experienced peers and mentors. Along the way, with deeper immersion into the dimensions of effective teaching and learning in general and, also, in specific for public relations, I came to appreciate the dynamism of teaching and learning *plus* the creation and administration of a PR program in higher education. PRE has proven to be far more rewarding than I could have imagined, and the next chapters address salient matters for starting out well as an educator—being one focused on PR.

References

Aldoory, L., & Toth, E. L. (2000). An exploratory look at graduate public relations education. *Public Relations Review, 26,* 115–125.

Canadian Public Relations Society (2010). Pathways to the profession: An outcomes-based approach towards excellence in Canadian public relations and communications management education. *Journal of Professional Communication, 1*(1), 211–241. Retrieved from https://mulpress.mcmaster.ca/jpc/article/view/96/51

Commission on Graduate Study in Public Relations (1985). *Advancing public relations education*. New York, NY: Foundation for Public Relations Research and Education.

Commission on Public Relations Education (CPRE) (1975). A design for public relations education. *Public Relations Review, 1*, 56–66. Retrieved from https://www.sciencedirect. com/science/article/pii/S0363811175800063

Commission on Public Relations Education (CPRE) (2001). *A port of entry: Public relations education for the 21st century*. New York, NY: Author. Retrieved from http://www. commissionpred.org/commission-reports/

Commission on Public Relations Education (CPRE) (2006). *The professional bond: PR education for the 21st century*. New York, NY: Author. Retrieved from http://www. commissionpred.org/commission-reports/

Commission on Public Relations Education (CPRE) (2012). *Standards for a master's degree in public relations: Educating for complexity*. New York, NY: Author. Retrieved from http:// www.commissionpred.org/commission-reports/

Commission on Public Relations Education (CPRE) (2015). *Industry-educator summit on public relations education*. New York, NY: Author. Retrieved from https://instituteforpr. org/wp-content/uploads/CPRE20Summit20Summary20Report20July202015.pdf

Commission on Public Relations Education (CPRE) (2018). *Fast Forward: Foundations + future state. Educators + Practitioners: 2017 report on undergraduate education*. New York: Author. Retrieved from http://www.commissionpred.org/commission-reports/fast-forward-foundations-future-state-educators-practitioners/

Commission on Public Relations Education (CPRE) (2023a). *Navigating change: Recommendations for advancing undergraduate public relations education: The 50th anniversary report*. New York: Author. Retrieved from https://www.commissionpred.org/wp-content/ uploads/2023/11/CPRE-50th-Anniversary-Report-FINAL.pdf

Commission on Public Relations Education (CPRE) (2023b). *Reports*. New York: Author. Retrieved from https://www.commissionpred.org/cpre-resources/

Coombs, W.T., & Holladay, S. J. (2014). *It's not just PR: Public relations in society* (2nd ed.). Malden, MA: Blackwell.

Crooks, A. (2017). Educating society's future PR practitioners: An exploration of "preparedness" as a qualitative indicator of higher education performance. In B. Van Ruler, I. Smit, Ø. Ihlen, & S. Romenti (Eds.), *How strategic communication shapes value and innovation in society* (pp. 1–21). Emerald Publishing. doi:10.1108/S2398-391420170000002001

Cutlip, S. M. (1994). *The unseen power: Public relations, a history*. Hillside, NJ: Lawrence Erlbaum.

Cutlip, S. M. (1997). The unseen power: A brief history of public relations. In C. L. Caywood (Ed.), *The Handbook of Strategic Public Relations and Integrated Communications* (pp. 15–33). New York: McGraw-Hill..

Cutlip, S. M., Center, A. H., & Broom, G. M. (1994). *Effective public relations* (7th ed.). Upper Saddle River, NJ: Prentice Hall..

Duhé, S. (2016). *The three pillars of PR education in the future*. Retrieved from https:// instituteforpr.org/view-public-relations-education/

Edwards, L., & Hodges, C. E. M. (2011). *Public relations, society, & culture: Theoretical and empirical explorations*. New York, NY: Routledge.

Gallup & Bates College (2019). *Forging pathways to purposeful work: The role of higher education*. Washington, DC: Gallup. Retrieved from https://www.gallup.com/education/248222/ gallup-bates-purposeful-work-2019.aspx

Hon, L. D., Fitzpatrick, K. R., & Hall, M. R. (2004). Searching for the "ideal" graduate public relations curriculum. *Journalism and Mass Communication Educator, 59*, 126–142.

Jain, R. (2017). Preparing students for the global workplace: Current practices and future direction in international public relations education. *Journal of Public Relations Education, 3*(1), 14–35. Retrieved from https://aejmc.us/jpre/2017/05/24/preparing-students-for-the-global-workplace-current-practices-and-future-directions-in-international-public-relations-education/

Kern-Foxworth, M. (2015). Introducing gender and diversity issues in public relations courses. In B. D. Neff & T. L. Johnson (Eds.), *Learning to teach: What you need to know to develop a successful career as a public relations educator* (4th ed., chapter 2.2). New York, NY: Public Relations Society of America. (Published in electronic form for download or on CD-ROM)

Kim, E., & Johnson, T. L. (2011). *Sailing through the port: Does PR education prepare students for the profession?* Retrieved from https://instituteforpr.org/education-preparation/

Landis, K. (2019). The public relations industry is too white and the solution starts with higher education. *INSIGHT into Diversity, 93*(1), 52–55.

L'Etang, J. (2012). Public relations and democracy: Historical reflections and implications. In S. M. Oliver (Ed.), *Handbook of corporate communication and public relations: Pure and applied* (pp. 342–353). New York, NY: Routledge. (Original work published 2004)

Pieczka, M., & L'Etang, J. (2001). Public relations and the question of professionalism. In R. L. Heath (Ed.), *Handbook of public relations* (pp. 223–235). Thousand Oaks, CA: Sage.

Shen, H., & Toth, E. L. (2008). An ideal public relations master's curriculum: Expectations and status quo. *Public Relations Review, 34*, 309–311.

Taylor, M. (2010). Public relations in the enactment of civil society. In R. L. Heath (Ed.), *The SAGE handbook of public relations* (pp. 5–15). Thousand Oaks, CA: SAGE Publications.

Tench, R., & Deflagbe, D. (2008). Towards a global curriculum: A summary of literature concerning public relations education, professionalism and globalization. Report for the Global Alliance for Public Relations and Communication Management, Leeds Metropolitan University, UK. Retrieved from http://www.globalalliancepr.usi.ch/website/sites/default/files/fedeles/Global%20Curriculum/Towards%20a%20Global%20Curriculum%20-%20final%20Feb1.pdf

Toth, E. L., & Aldoory, L. (2010). *A first look: An in-depth analysis of global public relations education*: Public relations curriculum and instructors from 20 countries. New York, NY: PRSA Foundation. Retrieved from http://www.commissionpred.org/commission-reports/

Tsetsura, K. (2011). How understanding multidimensional diversity can benefit global public relations education. *Public Relations Review, 37*, 530–535.

Vujnovic, M., Swiatek, L., Kruckeberg, D., & Galloway, C. (2023). What is AI teaching us about public relations education? In Adi, A. (Ed.), Artificial Intelligence in public relations and communications: Cases, reflections, and predictions (pp. 137–147). Berlin, Germany: Quadriga Univeristy of Applied Sciences. Retrieved from https://research.gold.ac.uk/id/eprint/34141/2/Adi,%20Ana%20-%20Ed%20-%20Artificial_Intelligence_in_Public_Relations__Communications_2023.pdf#page=137

Welch, M. (2015). Internal communication education: A historical study. *Journal of Communication Management, 19*, 388–405.

Wright, D. K. (2011). History and development of public relations education in North America: A critical analysis. *Journal of Communication Management, 15*, 236–255.

Xie, Q., Schauster, E., & Neill, M. E. (2018). Expectations for advertising and public relations education from agency executives: A comparative study between China and the United States. *Journal of Current Issues & Research in Advertising, 39*(3), 289–307.

Yang, A., & Taylor, M. (2013). The relationship between the professionalization of public relations, societal capital and democracy: Evidence from a cross-national study. *Public Relations Review, 39*, 257–270.

5

GENERAL POINTS OF TEACHING AND LEARNING IN HIGHER EDUCATION

This chapter gives a general and concise overview of selected theories and perspectives of teaching and learning that pertain to educational programs in colleges and universities.

Teaching is as much an art as it is a science. It is an art because of the personal and creative aspects that go into helping others learn well in subjects that matter to them. It is a science because of the ocean of scholarship about pedagogy (i.e., youth education) and andragogy (i.e., adult education) that demonstrates what, how, and why teaching and learning are so intertwined and can be so effective (or not). "Preparation" or "prep" is the work teachers do before they teach, making sure their personal frames of mind and plans for class are ready along with any material and activities that will be used. For teachers, key aspects that play into how they engage with students include personality, enthusiasm, leadership, management, relationships with students, and organization. For students, key aspects that play into how they engage with their teacher and each other include attitude toward learning, attendance, attentiveness, completing readings and assignments, note-taking, participating in class activities, asking good questions, and making appropriate and relevant comments. Students have implicit theories of learning and teaching that often do not fit with what teachers think, feel, and do. So teachers must explain what is going on, why, and the benefits to be earned. This dynamic between teachers and students is at the heart of education, which means having a basic understanding of teaching

DOI: 10.4324/9781003501817-8

and learning is so important to being a professor of public relations. From here, then, what are some useful and usable ways to prepare as a professor and engage well with students?

Managing Your Work

Being new to higher education and, especially, being a new professor at the rank you accept, there is a healthy volume of scholarly journals, trade publications, and full-length books with sage guidance about "the nuts and bolts" of effective teaching in all its dimensions in higher education. A few sources in particular are especially noteworthy, and having copies of them would be best because they are complementary to each other, especially as they matter to your preparations and expectations for any class. Boice (1996) presents 10 "first-order principles (FOP)" that are a great place to start because they are especially useful and valuable to new professors. For Boice, the FOPs are approaches to teaching in higher education that result in "documented changes of things that matter and endure in college teaching," producing "impressive outcomes" among those who have used them (pp. xiii–xiv). In summary form, the FOPs, which he also calls "rules," are covered here. Admittedly, the following summary is inadequate for what Boice presents, but the point is really to introduce the rules to get you started soundly and, especially, see how they intertwine for the better.

- *Moderate classroom incivilities with prosocial immediacies*—Misbehaviors can come from students *and* teachers, especially the latter. Top misbehaviors are students talking that disrupts class meetings; negative utterances or noises in response to teachers; students with very low emotional competence who unpredictably release outbursts that agitate other students or the class; teachers perceived as aloof, intimidating, or uncaring; teachers assigning surprise assignments; and teachers arriving late or leading class beyond the scheduled end time. Professors can manage classroom incivilities best by observing and understanding behaviors, arriving early and chatting with students before class, and using pauses, pacing, and checks for understanding of material. Reflect, then, on how well these things work for you and the class and adjust for the better.
- *Wait*—In students' minds, new information needs to be connected with old, existing information and cognitive structures. Waiting is a matter of patience in arriving at deep learning, not trying to get to the big idea or mastery of material immediately. Learning takes time. In this way, waiting is active and is key to students' cognitive processing. Active waiting is a student-focused approach to presenting material clearly, concretely, and methodically. Professors can engage in active waiting *before and during classes* by pausing reflectively to identify connections and pondering them and their implications.

- *Begin before feeling ready*—There is no need to wait until you have everything you need to do what you need to do. Taking initiative can spark inspiration that can result in discovery, invention, and progress on teaching plans. Pausing along the way to take stock of what you created and determine whether it is sufficient and engaging to work well for students is instrumental.
- *Work and teach in brief, regular sessions*—How do you eat an elephant? One bite at a time! The key is moderation. Working on, teaching about, or learning about something through short, regular periods of focused attention works better than prolonged immersion. The process for making sense of something for one's self and for others is easier to manage, resulting in better preparedness and learning. Do not be afraid of risk-taking that is based on sound consideration. Discipline in this regimen is key, especially at the outset.
- *Stop*—Know when enough is enough so that new matters can be undertaken. Stopping, then, must be planned so that cognitive processing and personal interests are supported and ready to re-engage next time. Stopping is as much a matter of temporarily wrapping up as it is priming yourself and students for what is next. Stopping a session early is not a bad thing either.
- *Moderate overattachment to content and overreaction to criticism*—Taking things personally leads to trouble, primarily (if not exclusively) to yourself. Everyone enjoys compliments and loathes complaints. Remember that everyone is a work in progress. Moderating your personal emotional responses to the spectrum of positive to negative experiences maintains perspective on what truly matters. Teaching everything you know is not important. Students already recognize teachers' expertise, and what they need and want is guidance to get them going well in a subject of field. When born out of love—love for others and for the profession— certain attitudes like patience, tolerance, perseverance, discipline, and diligence enable healthy, authentic reactions to yourself or others, simplicity or complexity, old information or new information, acceptance or rejection, graciousness or rudeness.
- *Moderate negative thinking and strong emotions*—The enemy of effective teaching (or whatever you do) is the adverse effects of certain thoughts and emotions. Dwelling on anxieties, regrets, and other negative matters undermines your mood, effectiveness, and relationships. Positive self-talk reverses the affects these things have on you. Recognize negative thoughts and emotions for what they are and why they are, then apply love, patience, tolerance, perseverance, discipline, and diligence to yourself in constructive and optimistic ways that improve yourself as a person and an educator-scholar.
- *Let others do some of the work*—Educators share knowledge as much as they help others discover knowledge. Knowing students' needs and wants,

especially in context of the outside world from academia, is essential to engaging students in their learning and growth. As a teacher, you can let go of some control and benefits of teaching by priming students with just enough background and a challenging problem they must solve. Other faculty may be willing and available to lead a session about one or more topics in which they are experts. Collaborative learning techniques are many and can foster inspired learning environments. Help from peers and students goes a long way.

- *Welcome learning and change*—As an educator, you are involved in teaching *and* learning, and you should learn about teaching and learning together. Scholarship about teaching and learning is a very strong and active area of research. It is full of insights, inspiration, and ingenuity about effective teaching along with deep learning. Whether on site or online, the literature on teaching and learning in higher ed can enliven your zeal for educating the next generation of public relations professionals.

- *Build resilience by limiting wasted efforts*—Successes will outnumber failures, and the latter must not deter your continued quest for the former. Thomas Edison said that, when inventing the incandescent lamp, he was a success as he found 10,000 things that did not work and one that did. Working moderately—not out of greedy intensity—can make the most of the work you do while being on guard for work that does not add the value you need or want. Disappointments and failures are challenges to rise above not collapse under. Learn from the triumphs and the tragedies and everything in between. Remember you have knowledge, skills, abilities, and experiences in other areas that can help you be the best educator-scholar you can be.

The watchword in Boice's rules is *moderation*. The principle of moderation is not specialized for higher education but, rather, is common sense. That is, each person must discern what levels of thinking, feeling, and action are optimum or most sensible to become the best educator-scholar possible. In this way, Boice's (2000) later book, *Advice for New Faculty Members*, is a great extension of his FOPs that are specifically oriented to new faculty. Most important in this later book is Boice's advice about managing work for the two other pillars of scholarship/creative works and service. In addition to Boice's work, a highly useful and valuable manual for effective teaching in colleges and universities is *McKeachies's Teaching Tips*, which is in its 14th edition (Svinicki & McKeachie, 2014). It features 22 chapters, some written by other education experts, that address essential matters in effective teaching in colleges and universities. The overarching matter to these (and other such) works is that, while you work out what and how you want to engage students, you must know and be honest with yourself in every regard for yourself and your students. Be a lifelong learner about yourself plus your fields of PR and education.

Of the many sources about what works best when teaching in higher education (see Appendix D), one particular book by Bain (2004) also is especially worth a look as you set out on a career as a college professor at any rank. The book, *What the Best College Teachers Do*, summarizes findings from Bain's long-term research about effective teaching in higher education. Bain's work also is very helpful with class preparation. Like Boice and like Svinicki and McKeachie, Bain addresses the full range of habits good professors have for all aspects of their work as educators. Two points about classroom management are well worth specific treatment here because it is in classrooms/learning environments that who you are as a teacher and scholar, what you do, and how you do it are on final display. The first point is the hallmarks of the craft of teaching: fostering good talk (conversational, not theatrical; good intentions); using warm language (inviting mental engagement; narrative in nature); making explanations (deductive or inductive views of the thing to elicit understanding); and getting students to talk (provide students with challenging things to discuss, dissect, discover). From these hallmarks, a professor should apply the next, second point of unifying principles for conducting class, which are as follows:

- Create a natural critical learning environment
- Have an intriguing question (perhaps embedded in a story)
- Help students understand the significance of the question (connect it to larger questions or raise it in a provocative way, noting implications)
- Encourage students to compare, apply, evaluate, analyze, and synthesize in addition to listening and remembering
- Answer the intriguing question (frame and present it as a well-formed argument; not necessarily the professor's answers)
- Leave the students asking, "What's the next question?"
- Get students' attention and keep it (the intriguing question or provocative problem is key)
- Start with the students rather than the discipline (backward planning for learning)
- Seek commitments (invite promises to perform at the level that is expected)
- Help students learn outside of class (not all material has to be covered in class, especially unanswered questions that are valuable to pursue)
- Engage students in disciplinary thinking (model and guide students through the ways professionals think about and handle matters of any kind)
- Create diverse learning experiences (allow students to channel their learning styles)

Notice how well all these principles are really essential to have considered in class preparations that would payoff in class meetings. Given this background about the nuts and bolts of being a professor, what actually goes on cognitively in teaching and learning? Those two things, after all, are the two sides of the same coin of education. The literature about both sides of that coin and the coin itself is extensive. In the little space of this chapter, a super concise overview of foundational principles of teaching and learning can serve well when getting into the particulars of leading PR classes.

Overview of Teaching Theories

When we look into what happens during one's education about something, we are looking especially into matters of memory and learning. The central question, then, is how do students learn, and how do they remember? (Detailed matters of motivations, behaviors, biology, and others, including the ones this chapter addresses, can be explored in Kauchak and Eggen [2014] and Slavin [2012].) The key to effective learning is time—time for memory to establish lasting neural pathways that enable ready and accurate recall.

Three principles are at play in memory: (1) crammed material (e.g., information, ideas, verbal knowledge) is mostly forgotten because its useful life is extremely short; (2) material distributed over time is recalled better, especially as it is learned over repeated attempts; and (3) material that is processed deeply (i.e., made meaningful by connecting to prior experiences, knowledge, attitudes, and emotions; experienced directly; and practiced on multiple occasions) is recalled the longest. Material that is forgotten easily tends to be what we receive passively, perceive as irrelevant, cram into memory, and never use again (Velde, 2003). Teaching, then, involves purposeful activity meant to foster the growing of neural pathways about particular things.

An important point to remember about learning is that brains change over time, both quantitatively (mass) and qualitatively (how it works). In this way, understanding where students are developmentally helps teachers to frame lessons and courses appropriately (see Paloş, Costea, Munteanu, & Drobot, 2010). Many theories of learning have been proffered, and certain ones are worth introducing.

Jean Piaget (1968) explains human cognitive development for children in terms of periods of figurative and operative structures, where concrete-operational thinking and, especially, formal-operational thinking are essential in the college years (Plymale & Jarrell, 1981; Velde, 2003). For example, students developmentally may have trouble with ambiguity—that topics or situations can have multiple answers (i.e., there are many more shades of gray than just black and white). Instructors help students learn how to negotiate ambiguity so they can ascertain the best answer from among many possible ones (see Klyukovski & Medlock-Klyukovski, 2016; Wright, 2019). Students, thereby, learn how to make decisions about what and how to do their best work within some learning-centered context/framework.

Particularly for college-age students, Chickering and Reisser (1993) examine seven developmental aspects that are instrumental but do not emerge sequentially. The first four aspects of the seven are foundational for the rest: developing competence, managing emotions, moving through autonomy toward independence, developing mature interpersonal relationships, establishing identity, developing purpose, and developing integrity (Black & Allen, 2017).

William Perry (1998) presents a theory of cognitive and ethical development for students during their college years. The implications of his work are that students' cognitive and ethical development is congruent with primary college goals, explains much of students' work quality, and reveals how effective teaching needs to respond to a student's stage of development (Black & Allen, 2017; Culver & Hackos, 1982; Felder & Brent, 2004).

In their model of cognitive development, Kuhn and Dean (2004) explain how people naturally move from absolutist views of knowledge (e.g., only one correct answer is possible) to multiplist views (e.g., options exist for answers from which the best can be derived). Teachers, then, guide students in coming to terms with ambiguity in the world, evaluate knowledge and evidence effectively, and make sound judgments (Black & Allen, 2017).

Leon Festinger (1957; Festinger & Carlsmith, 1959) addresses how people come to alter their perspectives (or not) when faced with cognitively dissonant experiences or knowledge (i.e., psychologically uncomfortable inputs). They hold onto their perspectives until they achieve cognitive consonance by reducing the dissonance, which minimizes the amount or forcefulness of inputs and maintains all or nearly all of the original view; avoiding problem inputs, which means ignoring such inputs so that the original view is not threatened; or accommodating the inputs, which means the original view is changed in significant ways. Learning, then, is facilitated by a teaching approach that imposes certain kinds and amounts of dissonance that is meant to inspire growth in a student's knowledge, skills, abilities, experiences, attitudes, etc. (Chabrak & Craig, 2013).

A prominent perspective on learning focuses on "learning styles." In this perspective, people arguably have one dominant way in which they learn, and these styles can be put into two categories. One category is sense-dominant learning styles, which involve sight (e.g., demonstrations), touch (e.g., completing an activity), hearing (e.g., lectures), and taste (e.g., talking). Someone may say, then, "I'm a visual learner, so I need to see what something means or how it works." Or someone else may say, "I'm a tactile learner, so I need to 'get my hands dirty' and work with the material." An auditory learner would prefer to absorb and process information gained by listening to sources about a given subject. An oral learner is someone who prefers to discuss a subject with someone knowledgeable. The second category for learning styles is non-sensory, and it includes logical (i.e., how much something makes sense and conforms to particular organizational schemes that pertain), social/interpersonal (i.e., learning gained by interacting with others), and solitary/intrapersonal (i.e., learning gained by engaging in material on one's own) modes. The reality about learning styles is that everyone learns through all of them, often in varying combinations even if it *seems* one style dominates more often than the others. In fact, research about learning styles is inconclusive about whether and how much dominant or preferred styles matter (Ellis, 2001; Pashler, McDaniel, Rohrer, & Bjork, 2009). Because learning is a matter of the amount and the quality of time, practice, and success one has with something, the more one "plays" with it in varying ways and successfully, the better.

Another view of learning focuses on the variety of "intelligences" people have. Gardner (1993, 1999, 2006) argues that people live and operate by eight different kinds or categories of intelligence that pertain to the variety of things people can do in any given situation and the particular needs for human development, creativity, and successfulness. The intelligences are:

- Linguistic (e.g., language/symbol creation, use, and misuse)
- Musical (e.g., appreciation, composition, and performance)
- Logical-mathematical (e.g., abstract reasoning and problem analysis)
- Spatial (e.g., relationships of things to other things in space)
- Bodily-kinesthetic (e.g., sensory-motor and rudimentary to advanced)
- Personal (e.g., developmental, "personhood," interpersonal/intrapersonal, and emotions)
- Naturalistic (e.g., comfortable and talented in the world of organisms)
- Existential (e.g., concern with "ultimate" issues, spirituality, and religion)

Additional intelligences have been offered for emotions (Goleman, 2005) and spirituality (Zohar & Marshall, 2000). Among them all, however, the key is not so much intelligence but, rather, *competence*, because the latter term encompasses much more of the intellectual, affectual, and behavioral facets they each embody individually and collectively. For teaching and learning, "multiple intelligences can serve as 'delivery routes' to personalize important cognitive and emotional processes underlying learning such as attention, memory, motivation, creative cognition, problem solving, and understanding" (Shearer, 2018, p. 4).

If learning is viewed as a personal activity that someone constructs for himself/herself, teaching is a means for facilitating learning through frameworks that encourage personal discovery that connects old and new ideas, concepts, information, and knowledge. Bruner (1960, 1996) presented this *constructivistic* approach as a theoretical framework that capitalizes on the way the brain constructs mental models to achieve organization and meaning for past, present, and, especially, future experiences. Teachers provide students with enough material to get them started. That material is structured within the context of the body of knowledge that is involved, including dialog, so that students are enabled to proceed in discovering principles (successfully and unsuccessfully, including rewards and punishments respectively) on their own but with the teacher guiding them as needed. The result is learning that occurs more deeply as students actively connect the dots between what they know and what they are coming to know, especially when extrapolating what they learn and filling in gaps in knowledge or information. Constructivism is active learning that begins with the questions that need answers (or problems that need solutions), which entails a process of investigation about why the questions matter and then leads to discovery of answers that are all the more personally meaningful and deeply understood than merely finding or being given the answers alone.

A Continuum of Teaching Approaches

Taking in these and other perspectives, and in very general terms, a continuum of teaching approaches is defined by its poles. On one pole is the traditional, "direct" approach. This approach is teacher-centered, using the metaphor of "the sage on the stage," pontificating about all that a subject is to students present and, presumably, enraptured by the professor's performance. This approach is authoritarian in nature, with the teacher in charge and students reporting to her or him in a top-down relationship. The teacher selects the content and disseminates information in lecture, and the students work independently and are mostly passive receivers of information and knowledge. Students survive by attending lecture, taking notes, reading, engaging in drills and practice, succeeding in memorization, completing papers, and taking exams. The other pole of the teaching-approaches continuum is humanistic. It is student-centered and applies the metaphor of "the guide on the side," who initiates investigation into a subject so that the students apply material from the course to achieve specific learning objectives. This approach allows for many degrees of freedom, choice, direction, and demonstration of knowledge. It also allows for collaboration, active engagement in material that is treated in context, and personal ownership of one's learning.

While there are teachers who operate on either pole of the continuum of teaching approaches, the reality is that, depending on many factors that matter to effective teaching and learning, combinations of teacher-centered and student-centered approaches are more often employed. The perspectives presented in this chapter easily address the needs of teachers and of students so that the experience of learning is fruitful for everyone involved. After all, everyone in the experience is a student, and the person who is orchestrating the educational experience is the lead student who possesses the kinds of credentials, background, and attitude that students and fellow educators and society expect.

A Question for You

What are your 10 most important principles for teaching and learning in college?

For myself, in my academic career I reflected greatly on what I learned about teaching and learning, which I summarized in Chapter 4. Much of the fruit from that reflection is in my philosophy of teaching and learning (a subject in Chapter 7), which has matured and expanded very much over the years to a point that it is stable now. After my first two years of being a PR professor, I developed my top-ten list of principles of college teaching. In so many ways, this list has been a guide to me in my prep work for my classes and is important to me to ensuring I lead my classes well. Perhaps these can get you started on your own top-ten list.

1. Bridge theory and practice, using problem-solving through case examples to help students make things meaningful by helping them connect the dots and begin with big questions on the way to sound answers.
2. Have high expectations and spell them out, including explaining them or reminding students of them from time to time, especially before giving and after grading assignments.
3. Be respectful of students as well as being fair and consistent in grading and in fulfilling the responsibilities of the roles of student and teacher.
4. Cultivate a positive learning environment in and out of class, including being true to my own positive attitude toward learning and teaching.
5. Coach students so they learn material mostly on their own and be a clear leader to keep the class on track, focusing on students' needs and enacting course policies consistently.
6. Find out and tune into students' expectations for the class early and explain the course design, objectives, and outcomes in basic and inspirational terms.
7. Establish a context for learning with objectives and outcomes for assignments. To this end, weave key concepts, information, and knowledge periodically through a course's content during class discussions and assignments.
8. Measure (formally and informally) how well students think the class is going, perhaps using a simplified SWOT analysis.
9. Recognize the general nature of students' disposition toward college— how do students think, what are their demographics, and what are prevailing values, attitudes, goals, etc.
10. Be selective about what I teach—subjects that "speak" to and excite me so that I can amplify my experiences, knowledge, abilities, skills, etc. I am just as much a student as they are, and I have the credentials to be the lead student, not just a teacher.

Even given this top-10 list, a few other principles arise in my work as a professor more often and tie to these. They are (in no particular order): Be yourself. Always enforce your syllabus policies consistently. Communicate high expectations and maintain rigor. Be compassionate. Admit mistakes, apologize sincerely, and make corrections right away. Remember that students are not looking for a friend but a friendly and competent leader for their learning.

References

Bain, K. (2004). *What the best college teachers do*. Cambridge, MA: Harvard University Press.

Black, S., & Allen, J. D. (2017). Insights from educational psychology: Part 3: College student development. *The Reference Librarian, 58*, 214–228.

Boice, R. (1996). *First-order principles for college teachers: Ten basic ways to improve the teaching process*. Bolton, MA: Anker Publishing.

Boice, R. (2000). *Advice for new faculty members: Nihil nimus*. Needham Heights, MA: Allyn & Bacon.

Bruner, J. (1960). *The process of education*. Cambridge, MA: Harvard University Press.

Bruner, J. (1996). *The culture of education*. Cambridge, MA: Harvard University Press.

Chabrak, N., & Craig, R. (2013). Student imaginings, cognitive dissonance and critical thinking. *Critical Perspectives on Accounting, 24*(2), 91–104.

Chickering, A. W., & Reisser, L. (1993). *Education and identity* (2nd ed.). San Francisco, CA: Jossey-Bass.

Culver, R. S., & Hackos, J. T. (1982). Perry's model of intellectual development. *Engineering Education, 72*, 221–226.

Ellis, A. K. (2001). *Research on educational innovations* (3rd ed.). Poughkeepsie, NY: Eye on Education.

Felder, R. M., & Brent, R. (2004). The intellectual development of science and engineering students. Part 1: Models and challenges. *Journal of Engineering Education, 93*, 269–277.

Festinger, L. (1957). *A theory of cognitive dissonance*. Stanford, CA: Stanford University Press.

Festinger, L., & Carlsmith, J. M. (1959). Cognitive consequences of forced compliance. *Journal of Abnormal & Social Psychology, 58*, 203–210.

Gardner, H. (1993). *Frames of mind: The theory of multiple intelligences* (10th anniversary ed.). New York, NY: Basic Books.

Gardner, H. (1999). *Intelligence reframed: Multiple intelligences for the 21st century*. New York, NY: Basic Books.

Gardner, H. (2006). *Multiple intelligences: New Horizons*. New York: Basic Books.

Goleman, D. (2005). *Emotional intelligence: Why it can matter more than IQ* (10th anniversary ed.). New York, NY: Bantam Books.

Kauchak, D., & Eggen, P. (2014). *Introduction to teaching: Becoming a professional* (5th ed.). Boston, MA: Pearson.

Klyukovski, A. A., & Medlock-Klyukovski, A. L. (2016). Instructor strategic ambiguity: Delineation of the construct and development of a measure. *Communication Education, 65*(3), 253–271. doi:10.1080/03634523.2016.1142097

Kuhn, D., & Dean Jr., D. J. (2004). Metacognition: A bridge between cognitive psychology and educational practice. *Theory into Practice, 43*, 268–273.

Paloş, R., Costea, I., Munteanu, A., & Drobot, L. (2010). The necessity to adapt instruction to the students' intellectual development. *Procedia Social and Behavioral Sciences, 5,* 323–327.

Pashler, H., McDaniel, M., Rohrer, D., & Bjork, R. (2009). Learning styles: Concepts & evidence. *Psychological Science in the Public Interest, 9*(3), 105–119.

Perry, W. O. (1998). *Intellectual and ethical development in the college years: A scheme* (updated & reissued). New York, NY: Holt, Rinehart & Winston. (Original work published in 1968)

Piaget, J. (1968). *Memory and intelligence* (A. J. Pomerans, trans.). New York, NY: Basic Books.

Plymale, S. H., & Jarrell, B. J. (1981). A comparison of community college and college education sophomores using Piaget's cognitive development model. *Community College Review, 9*(3), 19–21.

Shearer, B. (2018). Multiple intelligences in teaching and education: Lessons learned from neuroscience. *Journal of Intelligence, 6*(3), 38 [8 page PDF]. Retrieved from https://www.mdpi.com/2079-3200/6/3/38

Slavin, R. E. (2012). *Educational psychology: Theory and practice* (10th ed.). Boston, MA: Allyn & Bacon.

Svinicki, M. D., & McKeachie, W. J. (2014). *McKeachie's teaching tips: Strategies, research, and theory for college and university teachers* (14th ed.). Belmont, CA: Wadsworth, Cengage Learning.

Velde, G. (2003, June 3–5). *Teaching & learning 101: What every college teacher should know.* Workshops held during the University of Wisconsin System Faculty College, University of Wisconsin-Richland, Richland, WI.

Wright, A. M. (2019). *Let's be perfectly clear about ambiguity: Exploring instructor use of strategic ambiguity to enhance student work and learning* (Unpublished doctoral dissertation). Illinois State University, Normal, IL.

Zohar, D., & Marshall, I. (2000). *Spiritual intelligence: The ultimate intelligence.* London: Bloomsbury Publishing.

6

FRAMEWORKS AND OUTCOMES FOR TEACHING PR

> This chapter presents a very concise treatment of one orientation to teaching public relations that is highly appropriate. That orientation is constructivism, which was introduced in the previous chapter, focuses on student learning, and is enhanced by problem-based and experiential learning. This chapter gives guidance about helping students to learn well by balancing theory and practice that, in turn, advances the profession for budding PR professionals.

Are there "standard" teaching methods for public relations that any PR professor of any rank and background can use? The short answer is no; there is no one best approach to teach public relations. The better answer: There are research-based insights about sound teaching practices for public relations content, and this chapter will introduce them, building upon Chapter 5. In addition, there are research-based recommendations for what seem to be optimal constructions for public relations programs in higher education, and Chapter 4 presented pertinent example frameworks for the substance of undergraduate and graduate degrees in PR. Additional "standards" are those used to accredit PR programs based on their substance. The best one is the Public Relations Society of America's (PRSA) Certification in Education for Public Relations (CEPR), which is solely focused on public relations program content, learning, and outcomes that particularly blends the expectations from both industry and academia. Another program is the Association for Education in Journalism and Mass Communication's (AEJMC) academic accreditation for an institution's entire department or school of journalism, mass media, or communication in which a PR program may be offered, and

DOI: 10.4324/9781003501817-9

the accreditation criteria cover all of the department's/school's degree programs. The grounding, criteria, and process for these accreditation programs can be found easily enough online, and these programs can be useful as general guides for effective PR education even if a program does not seek accreditation.

The real point here is not to seek prefabricated teaching methods or programs for PRE but, rather, identify sound educational frameworks (i.e., orientations to teaching and learning) that pertain well to the work of PR educators and their students. Certainly there are ample ideas for teaching individual elements of public relations in sources like the *Journal of Public Relations Education*; the journals *Communication Teacher, Public Relations Journal,* and *Public Relations Review*; and the PRSA's book, *Learning to Teach* (Neff & Johnson, 2015). What is truly useful is a general framework for teaching and learning, like one from Chapter 5, to guide any PR educator in their own work with students. The key, then, for any orientation for teaching PR and achieving the intended outcomes, therefore, is this: bridging theory and practice that both the professor and the field possess for the benefit of students who want and need to master PR principles and practices for themselves. Concrete experiences, problems, or examples (i.e., the "what") plus abstract principles for effective and ethical action (i.e., the "why" and the "how") yields knowledge and—through successful practice and learned perseverance— mastery and excellence. In this sense, students are *constructing* their learning (i.e., knowledge, skills, and abilities) under the guidance of their professor. Both are mutually responsible for the experiences in a class.

Constructivism for Teaching Public Relations

Many times we educators integrate real-world experiences into our courses when we introduce real/realistic situations to address our classes, ask our students to review real/realistic public relations by others, or prepare realistic public relations discourse assignments. All are good things, and the kinds of realistic, hands-on work that students are involved in help them learn about the substance of the subjects we teach. In this way, learning is viewed as a personal activity that someone constructs for himself/herself, and teaching facilitates learning through frameworks that encourage personal discovery that connects old and new ideas, concepts, information, and knowledge (Bruner, 1960, 1996). More pedagogically (even adragogically) speaking, these examples of real/realistic public relations, such as the discourse examples we use from companies, are "educational objects" (Friesen, 2001) that serve multiple uses and have great instructional value. We instructors invoke kinds of virtual experiences based on those objects (including related discussion and assignments) that function at a constructivistic level and require students to actively solve complex and realistic problems using multiple perspectives and be aware of their own stake in the knowledge-creation process (Reiser, 2001, p. 63). Such experiences could be part of authentic learning tasks that reflect the complex nature of real-world, real/realistic public relations in which students would eventually engage in their careers.

A learner-centric bias is key to constructivistic education, whose principal proponent is Vygotsky (1978, 1986; also see Wertsch, 1988). According to Vygotsky and constructivist pedagogy, learning is based on human communication—"language, mnemonic techniques, formulae, concepts, symbols, signs, and so on" (Karpov & Bransford, 1995, p. 61). Learning, then, precedes the development of students' skills, and an instructor's guidance is similar to a master-apprentice relationship (Karpov & Bransford, 1995, p. 61); whereas, "socially shared activities [transform] into internalized processes" (John-Steiner & Mahn, 1996, p. 192). Such an approach is one that allows students to participate in knowledge building under the guidance of an instructor or other more competent person (i.e., working within what Vygotsky [1978] called their "zone of proximal development") that is at once social and individual. Learning is social as students collaborate with one another, and an instructor guides students' learning through structured activities involving complex and realistic problems and discovery about constituent aspects or basic skills (i.e., top-down processing). Learning is individual as students, through their discoveries, foster a sense of ownership of their learning and can monitor their own knowledge growth. Students are intimately involved in the co-creation of knowledge in the problem-solving process, which, as Vygotsky (1978) explains, is facilitated by "scaffolding." That is, students examine a problem in a real-life, authentic context; are given just enough instructional guidance to help them along in their tasks; then arrive at an appropriate solution on their own (see Slavin, 2012, pp. 222–223). In summary, basic tenets of constructivism are:

- Humans use language to learn, then behaviors develop thereafter.
- Humans learn best when lessons build one upon the other, using selected instructional objects (scaffolding).
- Humans' best time to learn something is at the moment when they are most open to possibilities (zone of proximal development); problem-based, "authentic" learning facilitates creation of such zones.
- Human education is possible through communication between instructor and student, where the instructor enables students to assume ownership of his/her learning through discovery.

An ideal constructivistic learning environment in courses (see Driscoll, 2005, pp. 393–402) would take advantage of the complexity of educational objects to demonstrate realistic and relevant situations from which students can dive into and learn how to handle at an appropriate level (i.e., beginner, intermediate, and advanced). Class discussions or small-group work would facilitate a communal dimension for learning, as students' perspectives on theoretical and practical issues are wrestled with socially and collaboratively. The learning environment would be stimulating and fun, as everyone encounters the subject collaboratively and actively, engaging their minds, hearts, and bodies in the experience (Ali & Cech, 2017). Students would be encouraged to entertain multiple perspectives to understand real/realistic public relations situations because multiple views of what can be done can stem from multiple models and research about what is effective real/realistic public relations. Students, in turn, can use their multiple perspectives to explain their responses in class assignments. Students also learn to take responsibility or "ownership" for their own development as knowledgeable real/realistic public relations folks and achieve the learning goals for the course. As a result, students become increasingly aware of their developing knowledge and can help themselves in constructing new "mental structures" about subjects and situations throughout their lives.

Old and new "mental structures" about subjects—especially in context—would be formed, explicated, and tested until satisfactory ones emerge (see Driscoll, 2005, pp. 387–388). The ultimate goal is that students develop knowledge about human relations and public relations practice and theory that can be applied in congruent contexts. More specific goals would focus on building students' abilities on matters like making sound ethical decisions, developing particular forms of discourse, and analyzing specific case examples of public relations. Important in this milieu, is recognizing that students likely will have varying abilities to follow directions. In my own research (Smudde, in press), students' inability to follow directions in college courses seems based on long-term reinforcement (since early elementary grades) of lessons about directions consisting of sequential steps and further reinforcement of those early lessons as students age toward college by other very common sources (e.g., how-to videos). The result is that many students are unable to process complex directions for addressing real-world, ambiguous, and ill-defined situations. In short, many students' mental models about directions do not work well in college courses. A scaffolding approach about successfully following directions that suits those real-world assignments ought to prove beneficial in helping students modify/expand their mental models about directions so that they can perform at the high level expected of them in college and, most important, in their lives after graduation.

Instructors would give students direction and feedback about their thinking related to both the theoretical and the practical dimensions of real/realistic public relations as dramatized in educational objects. In this manner, an instructor fosters a constructivist learning environment, where students are actively involved in the process that is framed by prerequisite skills and knowledge, an assignment, class discussions, and experience gained by personal engagement with the problem, question, or case. With effective contextualization of real/realistic public relations into lessons plans, students can confront specific challenges that require them to understand and apply certain concepts. Research on this kind of approach has demonstrated significant student learning in math and science courses plus non-math and non-science courses (Bransford, Brown, & Cocking, 2000, pp. 208–209). Selected educational objects facilitate students' learning by capitalizing on varied learning styles, and video is one example that emphasizes visual and auditory dimensions for critical thinking and application. The focus of this critical thinking involves problem-based learning (Jarvis, 2002; Jarvis,

Holford, & Griffin, 2000, pp. 117–118), especially in a constructivist approach about "real-life" situations, affecting both teaching and learning outcomes.

The constructivist instructional method emphasizes student reasoning, critical thinking, concept understanding, cognitive flexibility in weighing multiple perspectives, ownership of one's learning development, and self-reflection about one's knowledge construction. This approach allows students to bridge theory and practice in ways that empower them to—with the instructor's guidance—take charge of their own learning, achieve learning goals, "connect the dots" between what they have come to know and what they are coming to know, and construct effective ways of thinking about real/realistic public relations that will serve them in their careers as real public relations professionals.

Constructivistic Course Content Possibilities

Stories and case examples from the broad realm of public relations that we share in our classes in video or any medium are beneficial in many ways, especially at a cognitive level (see Freburg, Remund, & Keltner-Previs, 2013; Jaques, 2008; Pauly & Hutchison, 2001; Sisson & Mortensen, 2017; Smudde & Luecke, 2005). We engage our students in authentic problem-solving that requires various levels of cognitive processing at different stages in our real/realistic public relations curricula. By the time our students graduate, they should be well-prepared to solve the complex, ill-structured real/realistic PR problems that may have many solutions. Such an approach also can be referred to as involving "high-impact practices," which foster deep learning through multiple avenues for learning (Berrett, 2019). From individual writing assignments about situations, to the creation of complex real/realistic public relations projects, to the analyses of case examples, the problems we give our students approximate the demands of human relations in the "real world." As Jonassen and Hernandez-Serrano (2002) put it, "Novices in school are trained only to work on problems that are, by nature, decontextualized and well structured, while problems in everyday and professional contexts are complex and ill structured" (p. 68).

Realizing that the choice of media used for instructional purposes has an effect on cognitive processing, Cobb (1997) argues that the most efficient instructional media are those that "do some of the learners' cognitive work for them" (p. 32). This idea means that the way information is presented through a chosen medium gives the learner some amount of data to work from beyond what is in memory, and the learner builds knowledge about the task and subject by working through the problem-solving process at increasingly deeper levels. This "cognitive efficiency" with which someone works with information in a given medium is based on the rationale that, "while different media may not create different cognitive products, such as concepts, schemas, and mental models, ... they clearly do create different cognitive processes at different levels of efficiency (with regard to speed, ease, effectiveness). In other words, the form in which information is presented can determine how it is processed in a mind, and hence how it can be learned" (Cobb, 1997, p. 27).

When it comes to real-world experience gained through a higher-ed program in public relations, "experiential learning" has proven highly valuable and valued. In this realm of constructivistism are work-related internships (i.e., fixed-time job assignments for college credit or for pre-entry-level employment, preferably with pay), service learning (i.e., individual, group, or class projects to work with real clients to solve defined problems), community-based research (i.e., projects to identify, understand, and recommend solutions for problem situations), study-abroad programs, and student-driven research (i.e., independent study on topics of interest to students who want to investigate and improve a situation for the better) (see Moore, 2013). Private, public, civic, government, industry, institutional, or other organizations can be the sources of these opportunities. Experiential learning is constructivistic because it fulfills constructivism's principles and practices. The yield is students who have extended their knowledge, skills, and abilities beyond their courses through actual problem-solving *in situ*, in an actual public relations workplace, which means these experiences are most appealing to employers who want entry-level PR pros with sound experience that garnered solid results.

People Matters

Imbued throughout any constructivistic framework to teaching and learning for public relations is human relationships. Indeed, the matters of diversity to belonging are instrumental, from the gregarious to the reserved from ethnic background to socioeconomic status, from age to gender, from joyful to stressed, from the prominent to the marginalized—from these and beyond. Human relations are multidimensional, complex, dynamic, fragile, and integral matters for people living, working, and playing with other people and all aspects of the planet. Constructivistic learning, then, involves diversity and inclusion as relevant matters to experience and through which to grow as people engaged in the PR profession and society. Active learning about the diversity of people, ideas, contexts, and so on plus the need to be inclusive of multiple views, attitudes, cultures, and so on must be included in PRE (see Chapter 4, Table 4.1) so that students can connect better with each other and their professors during their education and then, later, connect with coworkers, publics, and others during their PR careers (Kern-Foxworth, 2015; Tsetsura, 2011).

Professors inspire students in their pursuit for intellectual, attitudinal, and behavioral growth, and problem-based lessons about human relations, particularly diversity and inclusion, are essential. Students must be able to truly see themselves as PR professionals. From the design of a course to interpersonal interactions during and outside of class, diversity and inclusion can and should be authentically modeled well from the professor and through learning objects. Keys to inclusivity are acknowledging your own implicit biases, creating and maintaining a genuinely positive learning environment, encouraging participation, offering support when students need help, using various examples and teaching strategies, and obtaining students' feedback about a class ("Inclusive Teaching," 2018). Getting to know students individually and collectively is important so that teaching and learning can be effective and fruitful. People may or may not remember something of what someone said, but they will definitely remember details about how someone made them feel.

Technology and Constructivism

Whether a class is held on campus or online, constructivistic, problem-based, and experiential learning is possible. For any classes, technology is a primary means for teaching and learning, as so much of what pertains to PRE is available in digital and analog media. In a constructivistic view, technology is an enabler of personal learning—students use technology for themselves and with others to analyze complex and realistic problems in a well-defined and relevant context, discuss and collaborate (i.e., whole class or small groups) on salient matters for deciding upon a solution, explore errors and missteps along the way, and benefit from instructional guidance when needed (Tam, 2000). From personal digital devices to printed books, material needed for public relations classes abound, and printed matter can be transformed into digital files so that they are accessible on electronic devices that have the capabilities to open them.

The technological promises and possibilities of online learning are well-documented (e.g., Allen, Seaman, Poulin, & Straut, 2016; Bailey, Vaduganathan, Henry, Laverdiere, & Pugliese, 2018; Means, Toyama, Murphy, Bakia, & Jones, 2010; Nguyen, 2015; Parker, Lenhart, & Moore, 2011). Particular keys to the constructivistic use of technology in online classes are allowing "distance learners to be more reflective, to give personal views on topics, to debate and argue their points of view, to question information given by the instructor and textbooks, based on personal observations and knowledge acquired elsewhere" (Tam, 2000, p. 58). Personal ownership of learning is the primary objective, done so in a community of learners who are connected to one another electronically but also intellectually and attitudinally so that they capitalize on the dynamics of individual and collective discovery under the guidance of an effective, sensitive, and expert teacher.

Online learning's greatest advantage is convenience; whereas, an online course's content is always available whenever students wish to engage with it. Online learning's greatest challenge is discipline; whereas, students must regularly focus on the material and truly absorb it on their own within the timeframe of the course. Different modalities for leading classes online are covered by the US government's definition of "distance education," which the Higher Learning Commission (2004) presents as follows:

Education that uses one or more of the technologies listed below to deliver instruction to students who are separated from the instructor or instructors and to support regular and substantive interaction between the students and the instructor or instructors, either synchronously or asynchronously.

The technologies that may be used to offer distance education include:

1. The internet;
2. One-way and two-way transmissions through open broadcast, closed circuit, cable, microwave, broadband lines, fiber optics, satellite or wireless communications devices;
3. Audio conference; or
4. Other media used in a course in conjunction with any of the technologies listed in items 1–3 above.

The Higher Learning Commission (HLC; 2024) also defines a "distance education course" as one "in which at least 75% of the instruction and interaction occurs using one or more of the technologies listed in the definition of distance education, with faculty and students physically separated from each other. The HLC (2024) also defines a "distance education program" as one geared to a certificate or degree "in which 50% or more of the courses may be taken as distance education courses."

Instructors structure online course content in ways that guide students through a subject with self-directed learning strategies and measure students' learning of the material through formal and informal learning assessments. At an individual level, the instructor's feedback about and grades for work completed in the course provide each student with a record of their performance and learning progress. Students, then, have great ownership of their learning as they work though the material individually with primarily (if not only) virtual interaction with the instructor and other students.

Artificial intelligence (AI) has become both a challenge and an opportunity for education (Vujnovic, Swiatek, Kruckeberg, & Galloway, 2023). Actually, a constructivistic approach to educating students about artificial intelligence (AI) is very appropriate. For example, pose a realistic problem for students to solve, asking some of them to generate content (verbal and/or visual) using AI while the others prepare their own content (verbal and/or visual), including citing of any sources that would matter. Then have the students scrutinize the two without knowing which content is AI or human, asking them to critique them for effectiveness and then identify which is which. Important in this activity is to extend the discussion to the ethical and professional issues for AI-generated content (see Buhmann & White, 2022).

Learning involves process and product—input, throughput, and output. Students individually can achieve similar results but expend different amounts of effort. Creativity is key, not merely following recipes to complete coursework. Course material, assignments, the instructor, peers, research, and personal knowledge and experiences are all resources for students' creativity. Students then apply their creativity to solve problems within learning-centered contexts/frameworks. Teaching and learning, then, involve "connecting the dots" between the *input* of theory and practice and the *throughput* of mental, psychological, and physical effort, including the instructor's feedback along the way. A student's *output* is the culmination of all the cognitive, physical, and emotional effort that went into its creation. Further learning results from reflection and discussion about how well one's work came out and later application of learned principles and practices.

A Question for You

> *What do think you would do to teach any class in public relations?*

For myself, because I had long wanted to become a professor, I collected many examples that I found from my own professional work, news stories, case studies, peers' presentations at conferences and meetings, and anywhere else I could get them. By the time I started teaching full time in higher ed, I had a deep well from which to draw, but some of the examples were dated or just not as usable as I hoped. Those problematic examples could be explained by giving a lot of context, but that extra explanation would take away from the instructional usefulness and effective learning. When thinking more about my students, it was obvious that examples with which they could identify (prominence or notoriety helps) worked better and more efficiently. So, with the counsel of my new academic peers and deeper reflection about the instructional possibilities of any example, I got better at selecting and applying examples in my classes.

The important point in this collecting of examples is recognizing the importance of what goes on in the "real world." Very important to that recognition is something about the nature of the profession of public relations and what goes on "behind the scenes"—what is the core matter, who is involved, what is the process, how are decisions made, why is an outcome successful or not, and whether the same or a similar approach ought to be used again. In this way, my role as a teacher was augmented by another role as storyteller. Problem-analysis, critical-analytical thinking, and decision-making drive the processes for the many kinds of public relations efforts on which PR pros work. It is never enough to show an example of public relations because that example is mostly (if not completely) the output of certain inputs and numerous kinds of throughputs contributed by many people. The story about the piece and its place in the bigger picture is important. In class, I could develop realistic, mock scenarios in which students would have to confront and solve similar problems so that we, in turn, could discuss strengths, weaknesses, next steps, and lessons learned.

Taking advantage of my personal experiences in industry and merging insights from research, my leading of students about public relations became more engaging. Not only could I present principles and practices, but I could also make them come alive and have students somewhat live them. Internships and service-learning projects would go the extra mile in application toward mastery. The principles behind problem-based learning and constructivism appealed to me immediately and were exactly what I needed to help me design my courses and their content for solid student learning. Admittedly, my successfulness in guiding students was not always great, but I could recover for the moment and certainly learn to make things better next time. Next time could mean the next class meeting or the next semester I lead the same course. In any case, "keeping it real" for students by sharing and guiding them through real or realistic examples of public relations has always gone a long way to preparing them for their careers by developing their knowledge, skills, and abilities concretely and constructivistically.

References

Ali, O., & Cech, N. (2017, April 8). "Yes, and" as teaching-learning methodology [Web log message]. Retrieved from https://teachingandlearninginhighered.org/2017/04/08/yes-and-as-teaching-methodology/?cid=nwsltrtn

Allen, I. E., Seaman, J., Poulin, R., & Straut, T. T. (2016). *Online report card: Tracking online education in the United States.* Oakland, CA: Babson Survey Research Group. Retrieved from https://onlinelearningsurvey.com/reports/onlinereportcard.pdf

Bailey, A., Vaduganathan, N., Henry, T., Laverdiere, R., & Pugliese, L. (2018). *Making digital work: Success strategies from six leading universities and community colleges.* Boston, MA: Boston Consulting Group. Retrieved from https://edplus.asu.edu/sites/default/files/BCG-Making-Digital-Learning-Work-Apr-2018%20.pdf

Berrett, D. (2019, March 7). How to bring "high-impact practices" to your courses. *The Chronicle of Higher Education.* Retrieved from https://www.chronicle.com/article/How-to-Bring-High-Impact/245836?cid=at&utm_source=at&utm_medium=en&cid=at

Bransford, J. D., Brown, A. L., & Cocking, R. R. (Eds.) (2000). *How people learn: Brain, mind, experience, and school* (expanded ed.). Washington, DC: National Research Council, National Academy Press.

Bruner, J. (1960). *The process of education.* Cambridge, MA: Harvard University Press.

Bruner, J. (1996). *The culture of education.* Cambridge, MA: Harvard University Press.

Buhmann, A., & White, C. L. (2022). Artificial intelligence in public relations: Role and implications. In Lipschultz, J.H., Freberg, K., & Luttrell, R. (Eds.), *The Emerald handbook of computer-mediated communication and social media* (pp. 665–638). Leeds, UK: Emerald Publishing Limited. https://doi.org/10.1108/978-1-80071-597-420221036

Cobb, T. (1997). Cognitive efficiency: Toward a revised theory of media. *Educational Technology Research and Development, 45*(4), 21–35.

Driscoll, M. P. (2005). *Psychology of learning for instruction* (3rd ed.). Boston, MA: Pearson Education.

Freburg, K., Remund, D., & Keltner-Previs, K. (2013). Integrating evidence-based practices into public relations education. *Public Relations Review, 39,* 235–237.

Friesen, N. (2001). What are instructional objects? *Interactive Learning Environments, 9,* 219–230.

Higher Learning Commission (2024). *Glossary of HLC terminology.* Retrieved from https://www.hlcommission.org/General/glossary.html

Inclusive teaching [Web log message]. (2018, October 30). Retrieved from https://tomprof. stanford.edu/posting/1684

Jaques, T. (2008). A case study approach to issue and crisis management. *Journal of Communication Management, 12*(3), 192–203.

Jarvis, P. (2002). Practice-based and problem-based learning. In P. Jarvis (Ed.), *The theory and practice of teaching* (pp. 123–131). London, UK: Kogan Page.

Jarvis, P., Holford, J., & Griffin, C. (2000). *The theory and practice of learning.* London, UK: Kogan Page.

John-Steiner, V., & Mahn, H. (1996). Sociocultural approaches to learning and development: A Vygotskian framework. *Educational Psychologist, 31,* 191–206.

Jonassen, D. H., & Hernandez-Serrano, J. (2002). Case-based reasoning and instructional design: Using stories to support problem solving. *Educational Technology Research and Development, 50,* 65–77.

Karpov, Y. V., & Bransford, J. D. (1995). L. S. Vygotsky and the doctrine of empirical and theoretical learning. *Educational Psychologist, 30*(2), 61–66.

Kern-Foxworth, M. (2015). Introducing gender and diversity issues in public relations courses. In B. D. Neff & T. L. Johnson (Eds.), *Learning to teach: What you need to know to develop a successful career as a public relations educator* (4th ed.). New York: Public Relations Society of America.

Means, B., Toyama, Y., Murphy, R., Bakia, M., & Jones, K. (2010). *Evaluation of evidence-based practices in online learning: A meta-analysis and review of online learning studies.* Washington, DC: U.S. Department of Education. Retrieved from https://www2.ed.gov/rschstat/ eval/tech/evidence-based-practices/finalreport.pdf

Moore, D. T. (2013). *Engaged learning in the academy: Challenges and possibilities.* New York, NY: Palgrave Macmillan.

Neff, B. D., & Johnson, T. L. (Eds.) (2015). *Learning to teach: What you need to know to develop a successful career as a public relations educator* (4th ed.). New York, NY: Public Relations Society of America.

Nguyen, T. (2015). The effectiveness of online learning: Beyond no significant difference and future horizons. *MERLOT Journal of Online Learning and Teaching, 11*(2), 309–319. Retrieved from http://jolt.merlot.org/Vol11no2/Nguyen_0615.pdf

Parker, K., Lenhart, A., & Moore, K. (2011). *The digital revolution and higher education: College presidents, public differ on value of online learning.* Washington, DC: Pew Social & Demographic Trends. Retrieved from https://www.pewresearch.org/wp-content/ uploads/sites/3/2011/08/online-learning.pdf

Pauly, J. J., & Hutchison, L. L. (2001). Case studies and their use in public relations. In R. L. Heath (Ed.), *Handbook of public relations* (pp. 381–388). Thousand Oaks, CA: Sage.

Reiser, R. A. (2001). A history of instructional design and technology: Part II: A history of instructional design. *Educational Technology Research and Development, 49*(2), 57–67.

Sisson, D. C., & Mortensen, T. M. (2017). Educating students for the social, digital, & information world: Teaching public relations infographic design. *Journal of Public Relations Education, 3*(2), 78–95.

Slavin, R. E. (2012). *Educational psychology: Theory and practice* (10th ed.). Boston, MA: Pearson Education.

Smudde, P. M. (in press). College students' ability/inability to follow directions: A synthesis of findings from 11 pertinent areas of study. In A. S. Munna, et al. (Eds.), *Transforming Education for Personalized Learning.* Hershey, PA: IGI Global. [April 2024 publication]

Smudde, P. M., & Luecke, J. R. (2005). Using *The West Wing* for problem-based learning in public relations courses. *Communication Teacher, 19*(4), 5–8.

Tam, M. (2000). Constructivism, instructional design, and technology: Implications for transforming distance learning. *Educational Technology & Society, 3*(2), 50–60. Retrieved from https://www.j-ets.net/ets/journals/3_2/tam.pdf

Tsetsura, K. (2011). How understanding multidimensional diversity can benefit global public relations education. *Public Relations Review, 37*, 530–535.

Vujnovic, M., Swiatek, L., Kruckeberg, D., & Galloway, C. (2023). What is AI teaching us about public relations education? In Adi, A. (Ed.), Artificial Intelligence in public relations and communications: Cases, reflections, and predictions (pp. 137–147). Berlin, Germany: Quadriga Univeristy of Applied Sciences. Retrieved from https://research.gold.ac.uk/id/eprint/34141/2/Adi,%20Ana%20-%20Ed%20-%20Artificial_Intelligence_in_Public_Relations__Communications_2023.pdf#page=137

Vygotsky, L. S. (1978). *Mind in society: The development of higher psychological processes.* Cambridge, MA: Harvard University Press.

Vygotsky, L. S. (1986). *Thought and language.* Cambridge, MA: MIT Press.

Wertsch, J. V. (1988). L. S. Vygotsky's "new" theory of mind. *The American Scholar, 57*(1), 81–89.

PART III

Approaches for Teaching and Learning Befitting Public Relations Education (PRE)

This section extends material from preceding chapters to present very specific ways of being a teacher and teaching well for student learning about PR. This section addresses assessing one's self as a PR educator, developing a PR program's curriculum and individual PR courses, and assessing the whole higher-educational endeavor that is encompasses in a PR program.

DOI: 10.4324/9781003501817-10

7

KNOW YOURSELF, BE YOURSELF

> This chapter addresses what it takes to honestly assess yourself, why and how those traits matter, and what to do about being the best teacher you can be. Key related topics include realizing your teaching persona, making the most of students' feedback about your classes, and constructing a teaching portfolio. An additional topic of participating in recruitment efforts is given as a culminating point about knowing and being yourself in ways that matter to others who want to study under you.

As you may have heard many times, "attitude is everything." Truly, attitude is linguistically constructed, central in human activity, and assumes guiding principles (e.g., orientation, world view, personal philosophy) are the foundation of an attitude that is behind an action. The first three chapters of this book are meant to spur greater self-reflection and self-understanding about becoming and being an educator-scholar in a college or university. For educators, attitude and action begin with a philosophy of teaching and learning. As Bain (2004) explains, based on his study of effective teaching in higher education, "Professors who believe that teaching is primarily transmitting knowledge may think that success depends on fixed personality traits [or intelligence abilities] over which they have little control ('some people are just born good lecturers, but I'm not'). Because others—like the people we studied—conceive of teaching as fostering learning, they believe that if they understand their students and the nature and processes of learning better, they can create more successful environments" (p. 174). Education is dynamic between teacher and students.

DOI: 10.4324/9781003501817-11

Your Philosophy of Teaching and Learning

Anyone who goes into education already has a view of teaching and learning. The question is, "What is that view?" The content from the preceding two chapters, then, becomes all the more valuable and useful on top of the content of the first three chapters. A philosophy of teaching and learning is a personal statement about what education is/is not, does/does not do, involves/ skips over, etc. Such a philosophy is personal and should be formalized in a document. A philosophy of teaching and learning fulfills personal and pedagogical/andragogical purposes (Brookfield, 2015; see also Montrell, 2003). The point of a personal philosophy of teaching and learning is not necessarily to crystallize principles in the theory and practice of education, although it can do that. A personal philosophy of teaching and learning also is not merely an exercise in theorizing, although it is largely theoretical in content.

A philosophy of teaching and learning is necessary and should include at least statements about the nature of learning; the centrality of language; the importance of process toward learning goals; the background, readiness, and intellectual and emotional needs of students; the difference teaching makes; the value of active and attentive students; and the love of being an educator (Leamnson, 1999, pp. 7–8). Additional statements should demonstrate your own reflections on your teaching, including topics that address evidence of teaching effectiveness; the value of and commitment to teaching; attentiveness to student learning and the differences among students' knowledge, skills, abilities, and backgrounds (O'Neal, Meizlish, & Kaplan, 2007, p. 3); views of how people learn, especially in college; your goals for student learning; ways of enacting your teaching goals for student learning though classroom practices; and learning how well you are doing (Ramani, 2009, p. 18). There is a lot to cover in this personal statement about teaching and learning, but you get to gage how to say what you need and want to say to make your philosophy real and useful for yourself *and* your students.

A personal philosophy of teaching and learning is truly a practical matter of "knowing thyself." After all, so much of what we believe about teaching is a function of how we ourselves learn (Haave, 2014). Various sources on the Internet, especially articles in publications like *The Chronicle of Higher Education*, *Faculty Focus*, and *Inside Higher Education*, offer advice about creating a philosophy of teaching and learning and being yourself in your teaching persona. A philosophy of teaching and learning is something that liberates one's attitudes, knowledge, experiences, biases, and behaviors. It liberates these things for an educator because it allows someone to know herself or himself *first*, and this is important to understand before designing a lesson or course and delivering it to students. A personal philosophy of teaching and learning also is liberating for students because it reveals the same things to them and serves as a touchstone for discussions about teaching and learning in life.

A philosophy of teaching and learning is not just one about particular "truths." It is a formal codification of what an educator values, believes, and acts upon within learning environments, which could be anywhere with anyone. Those reviewing philosophies of teaching and learning may evaluate them on the grounds of the person's goals for student learning and how well those goals are enacted and assessed, evidence of the person creating inclusive learning environments, and the structure, tone, and framing of the philosophy through the language used (see O'Neal et al., 2007). A philosophy of teaching and learning also can be specialized for specific learners and learning (e.g., first-year students; see Leamnson, 1999). The idea that learning is constructed linguistically is central to education, and a personal philosophy that establishes an educator's orientation toward teaching and learning goes a long way in their careful crafting of learning opportunities and the facilitation of learning among students who seek the instructor's guidance. Once you know your attitude toward and perspective about education through a personal philosophy of teaching and learning, the next step is to put that philosophy to work.

Enacting Your Philosophy

Your teaching persona is the manifestation of your philosophy of teaching and learning. As you think about it, the relationship between students and a teacher is a mutually respectful and trusting one, like apprentices to a master. A teacher demonstrates their values in words and actions, lives as a moral example to students, and leads students and makes decisions on sound ethical grounds. A teacher is a leader who is not authoritarian nor totally *laissez-faire*. A teacher serves best as a guide on a journey through extant knowledge and beyond, giving students (including the instructor) opportunities to discover what they know and are coming to know, especially through real-world/realistic learning objects and assignments. Teacher and students co-create the learning environment. *All are students ultimately.* Instructors, then, are truly "lead students" who fulfill that particular role because of their credentials and background to do so. So, as a function of your philosophy of teaching and learning, your teaching persona is thoughtful and intentional, not accidental or coincidental; it must be consistent and genuine, not variable and phony.

What can you do to realize your teaching persona? Good advice can be gained from successful colleagues, and useful tips can be found in published sources (e.g., Fairhurst & Fairhurst, 1995; Lang, 2007; Schaberg & Yakich, 2015; Shadiow & Weimer, 2015a, 2015b). A good place to start is building a rapport with students. You can do this by sharing some personal background about yourself, which shows who you are both on and away from the job. You could think about what you would want as a student, at least because you were in their seats once and can certainly identify with students' needs and wants. Reading analyses of today's college students can be especially helpful too, so you generally know something about how they think and feel (see Levine & Dean, 2012; Twenge, 2014, 2017). Consider the strengths of someone whom, to you, is a model teacher, then discern what habits of theirs fit yourself so that you might consider using them in your own ways. In this regard, genuinely be yourself, which should naturally differentiate yourself from your colleagues while also showing how you fit well among them. Also, remember the importance of humor because, when used skillfully and appropriately, humor can fulfill various rhetorical and intellectual needs, ranging from putting something in sharp relief to relieving tension or stress. Bring the outside world into the class so that what is going on becomes real and integral to the content of your course and material to a day's topics. Embrace experimentation in class when you are particularly inspired to try something with your students that fits a course and your learning objectives. Also, in this same vein, thrive on new directions students may take or inspire based on a day's class meeting.

Perhaps the most important matter of your teaching persona is communication. A key term in this area is "immediacy behaviors," which refers to the dynamics between a teacher and students (individually and as a group) that affect learning and other performance-related factors. In particular, as Comadena, Hunt, and Simonds (2007; also see Myers, 2003) show, three categories of behaviors matter most and affect student learning. The first is teacher immediacy, which means a teacher is personally focused mentally and emotionally on students while in their presence, using verbal and nonverbal communication that supports that presence and, thereby, reduces physical and psychological distance between teacher and students. The second is teacher clarity, which means teachers cover course content in understandable terms, in organized ways, and with definitive expectations for student motivation, learning, and performance. And the third is teacher caring, which means teachers demonstrate genuine interest in the welfare and well-being of students. An additional, partially mediating factor to these three is instructor credibility (i.e., students' impressions of a teacher as competent, trustworthy, and caring), which means students can give a teacher the benefit of the doubt if they have an occasion of being not as effective in the other immediacy behaviors (Schrodt et al., 2009). Throughout the course of a semester, the dynamics of any individual class will wax and wane—there will be good days and not-so-good days. Being effective means, while being true to yourself, you can manage the ways things ebb and flow for a class by using appropriate communication skillfully so that your relationships with students is largely positive and the learning environment works well for all (Worley, Titsworth, Worley, & Cornett-DeVito, 2007).

Student Feedback

Evidence of students' impressions of a professor's teaching is typically gathered through surveys given in each class at the end of a term. These surveys collect students' feedback about their classes. In this way, these surveys produce data about students' responses to instruction (SRI) and are *not* evaluations of any professor's teaching effectiveness or of a given course. In fact, ample research shows that students' feedback, both quantitative and qualitative, should not be taken as "evaluative," because, at best, they are truly descriptions of subjective student experiences in particular classes (e.g., Benton & Young, 2018; Berk, 2005; Hornstein, 2017). Indeed, the most important use of SRIs is gathering student feedback about their experiences in individual classes so that professors may choose how to strengthen their strengths and address any weaknesses.

Critical topics for research on SRIs concern their design, use, and validity. There are very real concerns about SRIs perpetuating biases (e.g., gender, race, implicit, explicit), overvaluing of quantitative data as the primary measure of teaching effectiveness, recognizing they are fully tied to individual classes and by themselves are not good predictors of instructor effectiveness, and being problematic in making comparisons among instructors and for making decisions about retention, promotion, and pay (Benton & Cashin, 2014; Boring, Ottoboni, & Stark, 2016; Franklin, 2001; Huston, 2005; Linse, 2017; Mitry & Smith, 2014; Spooren & Mortelmans, 2006; Spooren, Brockx, & Mortelmans, 2013; Spooren, Vandermoere, Banderstraeten, & Pepermans, 2017; Steiner, Gerdes, Holley, & Campbell, 2006; Uttl, White, & Gonzales, 2017). *Even so, giving students a voice about their experiences and listening to that voice is paramount.*

Overall, multiple sources of information are the most useful for both formative and summative evaluations of teaching, and most experts suggest the use of three kinds of data: self-evaluation, peer evaluation, and data about student experience. Open-ended questions about students' experiences in classes yield more useful information for instructors than other methods, and such questions are especially useful at midterm rather than solely at the end of a term (Flaherty, 2018; Signorini & Abuan, 2019). Obtaining students' feedback by midterm rather than at the term's end is better for both teacher and students because matters can be addressed for the students' and the teacher's benefits since there is still time in the term to do something, building upon immediacy behaviors. Ultimately, professors are ethically obligated to seriously consider using students' feedback to improve their teaching and their courses, perhaps including formal plans for making such personal or pedagogical/anagogical improvements.

Teaching Portfolios

Any feedback and, especially, demonstrated improvement in teaching is very valuable and necessary to show your growth and successfulness as an educator-scholar. Feedback data and analyses about your classes are, then, instrumental to your case about your effectiveness as a faculty member, and that case is usually made in a teaching portfolio. Teaching portfolios are highly useful, deliberate collections of material for an individual professor that show what, how, and why they teach (Pelger & Larsson, 2018; also see Carden & Smudde, 2015). Their utility applies to the person and to the institution. Murray (1995) explains that teaching portfolios document one's proficiency in teaching (i.e., classes led, assignments given, student feedback collected), function as organizing tools for and about the work they completed (i.e., teaching, research, and service), demonstrate to institutions the depth and breadth of teaching and learning that takes place (i.e., evidence that the institution's mission is being fulfilled well), and chronicle one's professional and personal development as an educator-scholar (i.e., examples of value-added and measured self-improvement efforts). Knapper and Wright (2001, pp. 22–24) present a list of the principal items used in teaching portfolios, according to survey research:

- A philosophy of teaching and learning
- A brief biographical statement to place the portfolio in context, including a thorough yet concise reflection on one's teaching abilities and effectiveness, especially showing how the philosophy is enacted and a plan for aligning behaviors and attitudes with that philosophy
- A statement about all teaching-related responsibilities, including advising extracurricular student organizations or programs that complement the curriculum (e.g., PRSSA)
- Any statements from students and alumni about how they benefitted from one's teaching
- Student feedback about courses and teaching and reflections about improvements made
- List of course titles and numbers, unit values or credits, enrollments with brief elaboration
- List of course materials prepared for students, including syllabi and example assignments, especially service-learning and civic-engagement projects
- Examples of effective teaching, such as student essays, creative work, projects or field-work reports, and awards
- Participation in seminars, workshops, and professional meetings intended to improve teaching
- Attempts at instructional innovations and evaluations of their effectiveness
- Statements from colleagues who have observed teaching either as (a) members of a teaching team or as independent observers of a particular course or (b) those who teach other sections of the same course
- Participating in course or curriculum development, showing actual contributions made
- Evidence of effective supervision on students' independent research projects (honors or not), master's theses, or PhD dissertations

Much of what should be included in a teaching portfolio is based on what case a teacher wishes to make about their record and successfulness as an educator, which can include scholarship on teaching and learning (see Huber, 2004; McKinney, 2013). Teaching portfolios are necessary for obtaining academic positions during your job search and, at different later points in your career, applying for tenure and promotions. Additional parameters for the contents of a portfolio also come from one's institution and, perhaps, one's field, and the contents and organization of the contents may be specifically proscribed (see Seldin, Miller, & Seldin, 2010). On balance, however, a portfolio summarizes someone's identity and competence as an educator-scholar and does so in compelling, evidence-based, and self-reflective ways that show competence and, especially, plans for improvement. Having a mentor and examples of others' portfolios are especially important because the process for creating a portfolio is long and involved as you collect what you need and organize the entire product.

Student Recruitment

The sum of everything you are and do is one important part of what students are interested in when they enroll in an institution. Sometimes students (and their parents/guardians) fastidiously examine colleges and universities and their programs, including finding out who is on a program's faculty and what they teach and research. In these cases, students are very intentionally targeting particular institutions because of what they are, how strong a certain program is, who the faculty are, and other factors. Most times, students (and their parents/guardians) identify institutions based on factors ranging from whether the parents are alumni, to proximity from home (near or distant), to available funding sources, to friends enrolling there. No matter what may interest any student and, ultimately, inspire a student to enroll in a college or university, the faculty matter in the decision. Students expect faculty to be experts in their fields, excellent in their teaching, outstanding in their service to them and the field, and approachable and friendly. An unstated matter for faculty, then, is the important role they have in recruitment of new and transferring students.

When students (and their parents/guardians) visit a campus, meeting and conversing with faculty is highly valuable. If a campus has days during the semester or summer when prospective students visit to tour the institution, get questions answered, and perhaps enroll in classes, meeting one or more faculty members can be a game-changer. Engaging in good conversation with prospective students (and their parents/guardians) is the key because you are taking care to make a personal connection with them (i.e., good immediacy behaviors). Through your presence, you show the humanity and the professionalism of being a faculty member, and that matters greatly to students who want and need to feel they are making the right decision to enroll. Depending on how a department handles recruitment efforts, being involved in and employing your PR skills can be a great asset to building and maintaining a strong program that carries a solid reputation on and beyond the campus. You help the students see themselves being enrolled in your program, they can pass along their good impressions to others, and they are eager to come to your institution.

A Question for You

What is your own perspective of teaching and learning, and how do you see yourself enacting it in a philosophical statement and in the person you are?

For myself, all my reading and research and thinking about teaching and learning in higher education led me to devise a means for keeping track of what I was learning and, most important, what stood out to me as inspirational and usable principles and practices for being a professor. What began as a simple list of concepts, insights, observations, and realizations from both scholarship and my lived experience became a detailed statement of what I genuinely believe and act on as an educator-scholar. My personal philosophy of teaching and learning has proven valuable for my students, for whom I always share it, so they know why and how I do what I do. My philosophy also has been vital for my career, as I needed to include it in my portfolios for being promoted to associate professor with tenure and, later, full professor. My philosophy also has been useful in nominations for teaching awards.

One of the most important realizations I had about myself as a teacher is that it is contingent on my personality, industry experience, my academic experiences as a student, and my growing understanding of teaching and learning. As a result, I found that certain values undergird my teaching persona. I do my work out of love for teaching and learning, my fields of study, and people. I believe we are all works in progress—personally, professionally, intellectually, emotionally, behaviorally, and spiritually. I am a model of enthusiasm, discipline, compassion, and friendliness. And I am tough and fair and like to have fun. Like anyone, I have good days and bad days, but most days are somewhere in between. Being highly self-aware matters in the moment with students and overall about myself—being something other than who I am at any time is ridiculous and a lie.

I came into teaching after many years in industry, and my knowledge and experiences in industry are key in my approach to teaching. In my courses, then, I apply many of the practices and demands of the "real world" so students can learn about and become prepared for how they will be managed in their careers. When students do well, I rejoice with them. When students perform poorly, I share their disappointment. Either way (and in between), I am here to help students in their learning. This vocation—teaching, researching, and serving in the field I enjoy—has been the realization of a long-term personal and professional goal.

References

Bain, K. (2004). *What the best college teachers do.* Cambridge, MA: Harvard University Press.

Benton, S. L., & Cashin, W. E. (2014). Student ratings of instruction in college and university courses. In M. B. Paulsen (Ed.), *Higher education: Handbook of theory and research* (vol. 29, pp. 279–326). Dordrecht: Springer Science+Business Media.

Benton, S. L., & Young, S. (2018). IDEA Paper No. 69: Best practices in the evaluation of teaching. Retrieved from https://www.ideaedu.org/Research/IDEA-Paper-Series#918426-faculty-evaluation

Berk, R. A. (2005). Survey of 12 strategies to measure teaching effectiveness. *International Journal of Teaching and Learning in Higher Education, 17*(1), 48–62.

Boring, A., Ottoboni, K., & Stark, P. B. (2016). Student evaluations of teaching (mostly) do not measure teaching effectiveness. *ScienceOpen Research.* doi:10.14293/S2199-1006.1.SOR-EDU.AETBZC.v1

Brookfield, S. D. (2015). *The skillful teacher: On technique, trust, and responsiveness in the classroom* (3rd ed.). San Francisco, CA: Jossey-Bass.

Carden, A. R., & Smudde, P. M. (2015). Using your teaching portfolio for career advancement. In B. D. Neff & T. L. Johnson (Eds.), *Learning to teach: What you need to know to develop a successful career as a public relations educator* (4th ed., pp. 551–563). New York, NY: Public Relations Society of America.

Comadena, M. E., Hunt, S. K., & Simonds, C. J. (2007). The effects of teacher clarity, non-verbal immediacy, and caring on student motivation, affective and cognitive learning. *Communication Research Reports, 24*(3), 241–248.

Fairhurst, A. M., & Fairhurst, L. L. (1995). *Effective teaching, effective learning: Making the personality connection in your classroom.* Palo Alto, CA: Davies-Black.

Flaherty, C. (2018, May 22). Teaching eval shake up. *Inside Higher Ed.* Retrieved from https://www.insidehighered.com/news/2018/05/22/most-institutions-say-they-value-teaching-how-they-assess-it-tells-different-story?utm_source=Insid%E2%80%A6

Franklin, J. (2001). Interpreting the numbers: Using a narrative to help others read student evaluations of your teaching accurately. *New Directions for Teaching and Learning, 2001*(87), 85–100.

Haave, N. (2014, June 2). Six questions that will bring your teaching philosophy into focus. *Faculty Focus.* Retrieved from https://www.facultyfocus.com/articles/philosophy-of-teaching/six-questions-willbring-teaching-philosophy-focus/

Hornstein, H. A. (2017). Student evaluations of teaching are an inadequate assessment tool for evaluating faculty performance. *Cogent Education, 4.* doi:10.1080/2331186X.2017.1304016

Huber, M. T. (2004). *Balancing acts: The scholarship of teaching and learning in academic careers.* Sterling, VA: Stylus Publishing.

Huston, T. A. (2005). Race and gender bias in higher education: Could faculty course evaluations impede further progress toward parity? *Seattle Journal for Social Justice, 4*(2), 591–611. Retrieved from http://digitalcommons.law.seattleu.edu/sjsj/vol4/iss2/34

Knapper, C., & Wright, W. A. (2001). Using portfolios to document good teaching: Premises, purposes, practices. In C. Knapper & P. Cranton (Eds.), *New directions for teaching and learning: Fresh approaches to the evaluation of teaching* (vol. 88, pp. 19–29). New York, NY: John Wiley & Sons. Retrieved from http://edweb.sdsu.edu/bober/montgomery/Article007.pdf

Lang, J. M. (2007, February 6). Crafting a teaching persona. The Chronicle of Higher Education. Retrieved from https://www.chronicle.com/article/Crafting-a-Teaching-Persona/46671

Leamnson, R. (1999). *Thinking about teaching & learning: Developing habits of learning with first year college and university students.* Sterling, VA: Stylus.

Levine, A., & Dean, D. R. (2012). *Generation on a tightrope: A portrait of today's college student.* San Francisco, CA: Jossey-Bass.

Linse, A. R. (2017). Interpreting and using student ratings data: Guidance for faculty serving as administrators and on evaluation committees. *Studies in Educational Evaluation, 54,* 94–106.

McKinney, K. (Ed.) (2013). *The scholarship of teaching and learning in and across the disciplines.* Bloomington, IN: Indiana University Press.

Mitry, D. J., & Smith, D. E. (2014). Student evaluations of faculty members: A call for analytical prudence. *Journal on Excellence in College Teaching, 25*(2), 56–67.

Montrell, G. (2003, March 27). What's your philosophy on teaching, and does it matter? *The Chronicle of Higher Education.* Retrieved from https://www.chronicle.com/article/whats-your-philosophy-on/45132

Murray, J. P. (1995). *Successful faculty development and evaluation: The complete teaching portfolio.* (ASHE-ERIC Higher Education Report No. 8). Washington, DC: The George Washington University, Graduate School of Education and Human Development. (ERIC Document Reproduction Service No. ED 405 760).

Myers, S. A. (2003, September). Becoming an effective communicator. *Spectra,* 22–25.

O'Neal, C., Meizlish, D., & Kaplan, M. (2007). *Writing a statement of teaching philosophy for the academic job search* (CRLT Occasional Paper No. 23). Ann Arbor, MI: University of Michigan, Center for Research on Learning and Teaching. Retrieved from http://www.crlt.umich.edu/op23

Pelger, S., & Larsson, M. (2018). Advancement towards the scholarship of teaching and learning through the writing of teaching portfolios. *International Journal for Academic Advancement, 23,* 179–191. doi:10.1080/1360144X.2018.1435417

Ramani, P. N. (2009). Writing a teaching philosophy statement: Why, what, and how. In M. Bart (Ed.), *Philosophy of teaching statements: Examples and tips on how to write a teaching philosophy statement:* Faculty Focus *special report* (pp. 17–19). Madison, WI: Magna Publications. Retrieved from https://www.facultyfocus.com/wp-content/uploads/2019/02/Philo-of-Teaching-FF.pdf

Schaberg, C., & Yakich, M. (2015, September 2). Essay offers advice on how to be a good and effective professor. *Inside Higher Ed.* Retrieved from https://www.insidehighered.com/print/advice/2015/09/02/essay-offers-advice-how-be-good-and-effective-professor

Schrodt, P., Witt, P. L., Turman, P. D., Myers, S. A., Barton, M. H., & Jernberg, K. A. (2009). Instructor credibility as a mediator of instructors' prosocial communication behaviors and students' learning outcomes. *Communication Education, 58,* 350–371.

Seldin, P., Miller, J. E., & Seldin, C. (2010). *The teaching portfolio: A practical guide to improved performance and promotion/tenure decisions* (4th ed.). San Francisco, CA: John Wiley & Sons.

Shadiow, L., & Weimer, M. (2015a, October 5). How do I make choices about who I am as a teacher? *Faculty Focus.* Retrieved from https://www.facultyfocus.com/articles/philosophy-of-teaching/how-do-i-make-choices-about-who-i-am-as-a-teacher/

Shadiow, L., & Weimer, M. (2015b, October 26). Six myths about a teaching persona. *Faculty Focus.* Retrieved from https://www.facultyfocus.com/articles/philosophy-of-teaching/six-myths-about-a-teaching-persona/

Signorini, A., & Aburan, M. (2019). Students helping students provide valuable feedback on course evaluations. *Tomorrow's Professor, 1700.* Retrieved from https://tomprof.stanford.edu/posting/1700

Spooren, P., Brockx, B., & Mortelmans, D. (2013). On the validity of student evaluation of teaching: The state of the art. *Review of Educational Research, 20*(10), 1–45. doi:10.3102/0034654313496870

Spooren, P., & Mortelmans, D. (2006). Teacher professionalism and student evaluation of teaching: Will better teachers receive higher ratings and will better students give higher ratings? *Educational Studies, 32*(2), 201–214.

Spooren, P., Vandermoere, F., Vanderstraeten, R., & Pepermans, K. (2017). Exploring high impact scholarship in research on student's evaluation of teaching (SET). *Education Research Review, 22*, 129–141. doi:10.1016/j.edurev.2017.09.001

Steiner, S., Gerdes, K., Holley, L. C., & Campbell, H. E. (2006). Evaluating teaching: Listening to students while acknowledging bias. *Journal of Social Work Education, 42*(2), 335–376.

Twenge, J. M. (2014). *Generation me: Why today's young Americans are more confident, assertive, entitled—and more miserable than ever before* (revised & updated ed.). New York, NY: Atria Books, Simon & Schuster.

Twenge, J. M. (2017). *iGen: Why today's super-connected kids are growing up less rebellious, less happy—and completely unprepared for adulthood (and what that means for the rest of us).* New York, NY: Atria Books, Simon & Schuster.

Uttl, B., White, C. A., & Gonzalez, D. W. (2017). Meta-analysis of faculty's teaching effectiveness: Student evaluation of teaching ratings and student learning are not related. *Studies in Educational Evaluation, 54*, 22–42.

Worley, D., Titsworth, S., Worley, D. W., & Cornett-DeVito, M. (2007). Instructional communication competence: Lessons learned from award-winning teachers. *Communication Studies, 58*(2), 207–222.

8

CURRICULUM DEVELOPMENT AND COURSE DESIGN

> This chapter summarizes how individual programs and their courses come into being through a curriculum-development process, resulting in a full program of required and elective courses that fulfills big-picture objectives from the student to the department to the institution.

When most people think of the word, "curriculum," they easily think about a set series of courses to be taken to earn some credential, such as a certificate of mastery or diploma. Curricula are, indeed, that, but they are more. Curricula must be learning-centered, which "requires we know our students as fully as possible" (Mackh, 2018, p. 9), while leveraging the resources of the institution to offer and sustain them. The reason why curricula are more than mere series of courses is that they come into being through thorough planning and analysis, are sustained through innovations, and are evaluated for successfulness, pertinence, and improvements. This reason points to the fact that any curriculum is developed through a concerted, collaborative, and learning-centric process that examines the what, how, why, who, where, when, and whether it should come into being and exist over time.

Curriculum Development Process

The curriculum-development process, as Mackh (2018) explains, can be envisioned generally as progressing through four phases, with each phase relying on the results of the previous phases: *identify* (conduct thorough research and empathetic analysis about students' needs for effective learning, generally among students and specifically for students who would enroll in a program), *ideate*

DOI: 10.4324/9781003501817-12

(brainstorm about what and how a curriculum could be), *implement* (create the best version of the curriculum possible and the resources it needs, secure necessary approvals, offer it, and measure its effectiveness), and *iterate* (use facts, experiences, and other relevant data to improve the curriculum to any degree to effect student learning for the better). "Curriculum development thus becomes a more holistic event, starting with academic content, learning outcomes, and intended learners, and accompanies by delivery mode, type of program, and assessment model as tools to achieve these goals" (Kaufman & Weiner, 2015, p. 105).

An institution's entire portfolio of programs can be thought of as a curriculum as much as an individual major or minor program in a department or school. "The purpose of the curriculum is to provide a set of experiences that will ensure that each student's development occurs in an orderly, balanced, and thorough fashion. The curriculum should provide both appropriate challenge and support to produce diverse types of cognitive, affective, and motor development and professional abilities appropriate to each person" (Gardiner, 2005, p. 94). Figure 8.1 illustrates how curricula nest from the program level (the smallest and dark circles denoting programs), to the department/school (the squares that encompass the programs), to the college (the larger squares that encompass certain departments/schools), then to the institution (the container of all the units contained). In this way, then, curriculum development involves a process very similar to strategic planning in business. The institution's top administration articulates the vision, mission, and objectives, and the academic units determine the ways they can live up to the vision, fulfill the mission, and execute on the objectives.

As Figure 8.1 shows, departments and schools can vary in the number of programs they have based on how they decide to address disciplines in their

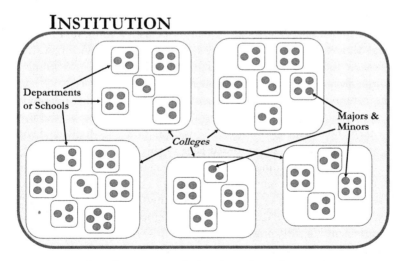

FIGURE 8.1 Nested academic curricula for a hypothetical institution

respective fields. For example, recalling Chapter 4, depending on the department of origin, public relations can be one program among others in a department of communication, English, journalism, or marketing. Alternatively, public relations could be a department that houses majors that focus on discreet disciplines in the field, perhaps ranging from message design, to communication analytics, to management. Departments and schools are organized into colleges using either traditional groupings in higher education or institution-based grouping rules or both. In a given institution, certain colleges (an alternative name for this organizational level is "division") can be larger than others because they house many departments/schools, as often happens with colleges of arts and sciences that can include biology, chemistry, communication, English, history, mathematics, philosophy, physics, psychology, and sociology. The size of colleges, in turn, also can be seen by the size of enrollments and graduates.

Using rules set by the university and, possibly, accrediting bodies, individual curricula in departments and schools are developed by committees of academics who teach, research, and serve in the field. A committee is typically led by a professor who has the vision and expertise to lead the effort to create a curriculum plan and has the support of the unit's administration. At the outset, the two most basic questions to be answered concern program or degree type and delivery mode. For the type of program or degree, a curriculum must be designated as a major (requiring the greatest amount of courses and credit hours toward graduation with a bachelor's degree), minor (requiring core requirements of a major but not all that supplements credit hours required for a bachelor's degree), sequence/concentration/track (a designated series of courses in a major that allow for a particular specialization in that major), certificate (a highly focused and short series of courses in a specialized area of a discipline to achieve a credential of proficiency), professional (a program of courses designed to support development of professionals in a discipline, perhaps useful to maintain licensure or accreditation), or graduate (a plan of courses leading to a master's or doctoral degree). For mode of delivery, courses would be provided for students face-to-face, fully online, hybrid/blended, or some form of synchronous or asynchronous means (Kaufman & Weiner, 2015, p. 105).

The committee developing a curriculum works to create a program that fits within the general framework for all curricula required by the institution, which aligns with the institution's vision and mission. Individual courses in a curriculum, as will be addressed later in this chapter, must uphold certain requirements, depending on various factors ranging from being purpose-based (e.g., labs, lectures, seminars, internships) to being government-required (e.g., teacher certification or professional licensure). The curriculum must also address matters of outside accreditation organizations when it matters, such as the requirements for a PR program being CEPR by the PRSA. Curricula, once approved by their individual academic units, undergo reviews at the college level then the university level to ensure the programs meet all pertinent requirements and students' informational needs. Once fully and finally approved, the curriculum can be enacted, including its evaluation mechanisms.

Lattuca and Stark (2009) show that any curriculum, which emerges through an institution's system based on the social, cultural, and historical context, is "an academic plan [that]…identif[ies] the critical decision points that, if effectively addressed, will enhance the academic experience of students" (p. 4). The development of a curriculum plan must, according to Lattuca and Stark, present a solid argument for it that substantiates:

1. PURPOSES: knowledge, skills, and attitudes to be learned.
2. CONTENT: subject matter selected to convey specific knowledge, skills, and attitudes.
3. SEQUENCE: an arrangement of the subject matter and experiences intended to lead to specific outcomes for learners.
4. LEARNERS: how the plan will address a specific group of learners.
5. INSTRUCTIONAL PROCESSES: the instructional activities by which learning may be achieved.
6. INSTRUCTIONAL RESOURCES: the [people, technology,] materials and settings to be used in the learning process.
7. EVALUATION: the strategies used to determine whether decisions about the elements of the academic plan are optimal.
8. ADJUSTMENT: enhancements to the plan based on experience and evaluation (pp. 4–5).

These eight elements are material to the substance of any curriculum that is designed, and the resulting curriculum is necessarily contingent on internal and, especially, external forces. Lattuca and Stark further explain that internal and external forces are at play. Internal forces are present on two levels: (1) institution, which includes vision, mission, resources, and governance; and (2) unit, which includes faculty, student body's characteristics, and discipline/field advances (especially with trends in industry, scholarship, and teaching). External forces include market pressures in higher education, existing examples of curricula (competitors, scholarship, and accreditors), government requirements and regulations, and organizations serving particular disciplines/fields. For public relations, curricula also should consider the recommendations from reports shown in Chapter 4 and give particular attention to matters of enrollment demand, diversity and inclusion (Kern-Foxworth, 2015; Landis, 2019; Tsetsura, 2011), service and experiential learning (Moore, 2013), civic engagement (Woolard, 2017), ethics and law (Gower, 2008), and leadership and business management (Smudde, 2023).

When curricula are developed and implemented with student learning as their nexus, the benefits are that students know what to expect and achieve so they can organize their time and work, anyone can know a curriculum's objectives meaningfully, learning can be measured, courses can be revised or created accordingly, and instructors are guided in their teaching (Hubball & Burt, 2004, p. 53). The enactment of a curriculum through the work of faculty and unit administration yields the proof of its successfulness. Evaluating a curriculum's outcomes, then, based on achieving student-learning objectives in individual courses and, thereby, the whole curriculum, plus other measures (e.g., alumni career performance) provides data about which adjustments in any or all eight matters in the plan should be made for improvements. This topic of evaluation, also referred to as assessment, is the focus of the next chapter.

Instructional Design for Courses

At this point, the development of individual courses for a curriculum is important to address as a matter of "instructional design." Instructional design "is a discipline in which practitioners constantly look to the findings of other disciplines (e.g., cognitive psychology, communication) to study and improve methods of developing, delivering, and evaluating instruction and instructional processes" (Brown & Green, 2011, p. 5). At a personal level, instructional design also enables one to apply their personal philosophy toward effective teaching and learning about specific material. There are multiple models for instructional design, and educators choose to use the one that suits their needs best. Because instructional design models vary in kind and in usability, it is appropriate to account for the common ground among all models. This common ground is captured in the metamodel, "ADDIE." This acronym stands for each of the five phases of instructional design and "is actually a means for describing the essential components of *any* instructional design model" (Brown & Green, 2011, p. 10; also see Bichelmeyer, 2005; Molenda, 2003, 2004; Peterson, 2003; Svinicki & McKeachie, 2014). A thorough and useful explanation of the ADDIE model is Welty's (2007), which is the basis for this application of the model.

The first phase of the ADDIE metamodel is *analyze*. This phase "identifies a performance gap" between what students actually know and what they must or should know but do not. The best way to begin thinking about closing the gap is to use an example course: compare students' current competency in PR writing to industry demands (e.g., Lane & Johnston, 2016). Research on and resources for PR writing abound, and an educator can lean on them, their own knowledge and experience, plus the counsel of industry professionals. The PRE reports summarized in Chapter 4 would be especially useful here. Depending on where in a curriculum sequence a particular course fits, analysis should consider prior learning and experience students would have and not have coming into the course under development/revision. In this phase, too, is the need to consider the mode of delivery—face-to-face, online, blended, hybrid, etc.—which matters in all the following phases. Another important aspect of this phase is envisioning a dialectic learning environment where students and teacher collaborate, and where students and the teacher identify with each other and the subject matter of the principles, practices, and expectations for writing in the PR industry. For example, a beginning PR writing course, especially designed constructivistically, would address certain matters differently or instead of those in an advanced writing course. Specific data and colleagues' opinions about student performance in relevant courses (especially prerequisites) will be needed to gauge the span of the gap between students' competence and industry demands.

The second phase of the ADDIE metamodel is *design*, and it involves "a planned approach to addressing the performance gap [that] is outlined and approved" because "the learning product [fits] into the larger curriculum." The best way to engage in this phase is to use the findings from the analysis phase to specify desired learning outcomes from the course in PR writing and work backwards. Fink's (2013) approach to the design phase is especially useful. His "backward design" process includes five steps: (1) identify situational factors among the subject, students, teacher, and environment that can help or hurt learning; (2) establish objectives for student learning by a course's end (i.e., addressing the six areas of foundational knowledge, application, integration, human dimensions, caring, and learning how to learn) so that the combination of these goals results in significant learning; (3) consider feedback and assessment procedures to guide students during their learning; (4) find appropriate teaching and learning activities that will move the students progressively and significantly toward fulfilling learning objectives (i.e., the richer the learning the better); and (5) integrate all these components into a system that contribute to and support each other. One key result from this design phase should be a draft syllabus and schedule for the course that lays out the range of things that will be covered and completed (see Appendix B). Institutions should have a policy about the minimum content for a syllabus, and such content would include the following:

- Course number, name, and catalog description
- Instructor's name, office hours and location, and contact information
- Overview of the course
- Learning objectives
- Instructional material needed (textbook, readings, technology, etc.)
- Reasonable accommodations for documented disabilities or medical/ mental health condition
- Assignments summary
- Course schedule
- Evaluation approach for final grades
- Syllabus change policy
- Policies about attendance, plagiarism, and others as needed

FIGURE 8.2 Bloom's updated taxonomy

Instrumental in this phase is Bloom's (1956) taxonomy for organizing learning objectives from the most basic to most complex (Mackh, 2018). Figure 8.2 illustrates the taxonomy, which is an updated version of the original he created in 1956 (see Anderson et al., 2001). The taxonomy's value in course design is, parallel to and complementary with Fink's (2013) taxonomy that will be addressed in Chapter 9, its usefulness in writing specific and measurable learning objectives based on the level of knowledge, skills, and abilities students are to build in a course. At each level in Bloom's taxonomy (see Figure 8.2), there are particular verbs that would be used to express the specific way learning outcomes would be recognized when measuring student learning through assignments. In the figure sample, verbs are listed to spur the writing of learning objectives. (Larger lists of verbs that are helpful in writing objectives are findable online too.) For example, essential or foundational learning is at the most basic level of "remembering" certain things. As Figure 8.2 shows, effective learning objectives express the learning outcomes in particular terms that pertain to memory and recall. The next level up is "understanding," which requires more complex cognitive activity when constructing meaning about something and, thereby, can be expressed in a learning objective that focuses on students truly "getting it." The approach is very similar as you go up success levels in the taxonomy, realizing that the knowledge, skills, and abilities built in lower levels are essential for extending them and gaining success in higher levels. The trick is making sure the levels targeted for student learning are appropriate. Not every level in the taxonomy may be appropriate for every course, so an instructor must diligently begin with the ultimate learning outcomes for a curriculum sought and work backwards to connect them with the course's learning objectives stated, lessons conducted, and assignments completed.

Meeting learning objectives through well-designed learning objects is next in the design phase. Specific lessons and assignments that build upon the lessons are necessary to give students opportunities to play with the course's content and learn what they should. The objectives point to the outcomes that students should realize through their learning under your guidance with instructional material. For a lesson, begin with what students already know and progressively build upon it (called "scaffolding") with new knowledge, skills, and abilities that pertain through combinations of lecture, discussion, case analysis, practice/experiment, or other method. In scaffolding (Mackh, 2018, p. 108), after a teacher situates a learning object in context, they *demonstrate* a topic through a model or example the students are to understand; *facilitates* student learning through a guided activity that can be done individually, in pairs, or in small groups (see Barkley [2010] and Barkley, Cross, & Major [2005] for examples); then *evaluates* how well students did in the activity that, if applied, leads to an out-of-class assignment. For example, real-world or realistic writing assignments and work situations reveal dimensions about the dynamics and demands of public relations writing that may otherwise remain hidden (especially because of any ingrained bad habits) and illustrates the importance of particular points or orientations about the roles of professional writing in today's organizations through a story or two that relates. An excellent source of examples for leading particular topic-focused lessons is given in Neff and Johnson (2015).

The mode of delivery, as decided in the analyze phase, is addressed in this design phase. For example, leading a class face-to-face on campus will require very different approaches than leading a class that is fully online. Designing a course for any mode still would follow the ADDIE model, yet particular guidance still would be needed for online learning. An excellent framework for designing courses for effective online learning is offered by Quality Matters (QM, 2018), which is "an international, U.S.-based, non-profit organization specializing in standards, processes and professional development for quality assurance in online and blended learning" (p. 2). By applying research about effective online teaching and learning, QM has identified best practices (called "standards") for online and blended courses in higher education that are applied according to rubrics that guide course development, facilitate peer reviews of online courses, and culminate in certification in online course design. Faculty may enroll in QM programs where they are offered, which can be directly on institution's campuses.

The third phase of the ADDIE metamodel is *develop*, which includes all activity needed to bring a learning product (i.e., anything from a whole course to individual assignments) into being for an educational opportunity. With the syllabus in hand, the teacher devises the actual learning objects/products, from lectures, class activities, and experiences to quizzes/tests, assignments, and scoring rubrics. Organizing course material into modules or a similar approach is a good way to help students in their work and learning while you stay on track. Given the mode of delivery, this phase can be lengthy because it involves the development and revision of the very material the teacher and students will use based on the results of the analyze and design phases (Mackh, 2018). Certain revisions of the syllabus and course content may be necessary as the teacher considers situational constraints that may affect the course design and schedule. For example, the naming of a concept can be key to helping students unlock the secrets of the writing process in industry settings, and technical terms can similarly help students become competent in analyzing the writing process as critics and participants. The essence of the writing process in organizations can be revealed through various kinds of examples, testimonials, or cases. Framing selected public relations actions can help students understand their own and organizations' orientations toward writing and see how those orientations can be strengthened or corrected. Assignments must address matters of form so that students understand and apply the conventions for PR discourse meant for various purposes and audiences.

The fourth phase of the ADDIE metamodel is *implement*. This phase is the enactment of learning products between a teacher and students. Given what was prepared for the chosen mode of delivery, all the planning and creating comes together and should pay off in learning that moves students closer to fulfilling one or more learning objectives. In a PR writing class, lecture and class discussion or activities lead to new levels of knowing about industry expectations in process and people management, writing quality, text production and distribution, reader usability, and continuous improvement procedures for future texts. Assignments specifically challenge students to think about and solve specific problems in one or more of these areas, and each assignment builds in complexity and challenge from its predecessors. Assignments should require students to demonstrate their command of subject matter by using the key terms and concepts in context. Assignments should also challenge students to demonstrate their command of and problem-solving abilities for particular writing situations and how audiences would respond to the finished work.

The final phase of the ADDIE metamodel is *evaluate*, and it involves measuring and analyzing the findings about both student learning and the effectiveness/ appropriateness of a learning product. Knowledge about how well students are learning is gained through various methods, such as direct/indirect, authentic, and embedded assessment techniques in courses and programs (cf. Allen, 2004; Barkley & Major, 2016; Kuh et al., 2015). Based on that knowledge, if things could be better, educators can make adjustments; and if things work well, educators know where to capitalize on success. Scoring rubrics can be used for all assignments to present assessment criteria, such as specific skill sets, effectiveness expectations, and other requirements with numerical values to indicate varied levels of successful-ness in meeting learning expectations. When coupled with a teacher's written and oral comments, these rubrics are useful tools for showing students how well they are learning on assignment specific dimensions and according to course-general learning goals. Such assessments of student proficiency should result in significant learning during and outside of class, giving students ways to improve their own work, discuss their performance with the teacher, and talk with their peers about the work they are doing. Matters of form, following instructions, and applying discourse conventions would show how well students are progressing in their mastery of course content through assignments, class participation, etc.

Education is not an *either-or* business; it is a *both-and* business (Berry, 2010). Very broadly speaking, the predominant matters of education concern purpose, curriculum, teachers' and students' roles, learning environment, and measure-ments of teaching and learning effectiveness. The first matter of *purpose* varies, depending on multiple factors, and must be defined for the process of designing curricula and individual courses. One example of purpose is to bridge theory and practice. Other purposes can be more specific and detailed, such as those that enable students to develop appropriate research methods to analyze given communication situations. The second matter of *curriculum* concerns what will be taught and learned in a program of courses leading to a degree. The third matter of *teachers' and students' roles* focuses on how the two will work together and the personal expectations in the educational enterprise in which they engage themselves. The fourth matter of the *learning environment* covers the setting and structure in which a teacher and the students will engage in learn-ing, and that environment is not restricted to a classroom, branching off to any formal or informal out-of-class engagement in learning. The fifth matter of *measuring teaching and learning* (see Chapter 9) concerns obtaining feedback about teachers teaching and students learning. Such assessments can span the levels of micro (person) to the mezzo (program curriculum or department) to the macro (institution).

A Question for You

What are your expectations for being involved in the development of a public relations curriculum and individual PR courses?

For myself, my only sense of a curriculum in higher education came from the majors I completed as an undergraduate and my degree programs for my master's and doctoral degrees. So, I knew my departments had collections of courses, where certain ones were arranged in definitive ways to make up particular programs of study for the degree levels offered. There also were coursework and credit-hour requirements to be met at the university level and the department level. So, the catalog of courses that my universities published and the supplemental material from my departments guided me in what I needed to do to graduate. I had no idea about how curricula and their courses were developed and enacted before I became a full-time academic.

Since I moved into academia full time in 2002, I learned how thorough the development process is for curricula and individual courses, including making changes in existing ones let alone creating new ones. In my academic career, I developed courses myself, benefitting from the guidance of my department chairs, senior faculty, and my own research and education in teaching and learning about what I needed to do to have successful course designs. As I progressed in my academic career, I worked on curriculum review committees at the department, college, and university levels. Each level examines curriculum and course proposals according to the purview it has, but they all tend to the same matters about what a curriculum or new/revised course must have, say, and achieve. In these committees, I learned well about the organizational processes. Even though an institution's bureaucracy can seem unwieldy, these processes are truly meant to be helpful at every step of the way and are reasonable and, occasionally, time consuming.

The more I developed as an educator-scholar and designed and reviewed curricula and courses, the more I came to see the wisdom of the work and the process involved. The parallels with strategic planning and resource allocations that are undertaken in industry were very helpful in doing the right things for student learning, the departments, and the institutions for which I worked. Clearly, the analytical thinking and transferrable skills from industry, plus my own work in curricula at various levels, paid off well.

References

Allen, M. J. (2004). *Assessing academic programs in higher education.* Bolton, MA: Anker.

Anderson, L. W., Krathwohl, D. R., Airasian, P. W., Cruikshank, K. A., Mayer, R. E., Pintrich, P. R., Raths, J., & Wittrock, M. C. (Eds.) (2001). *A taxonomy of learning, teaching, and assessing: A revision of Bloom's taxonomy of educational objectives* (Complete ed.). New York, NY: Longman.

Barkley, E. F. (2010). *Student engagement techniques: A handbook for college faculty.* San Francisco, CA: Jossey-Bass.

Barkley, E. F., Cross, K. P., & Major, C. H. (2005). *Collaborative learning techniques: A handbook for college faculty.* San Francisco, CA: Jossey-Bass.

Barkley, E. F., & Major, C. H. (2016). *Learning assessment techniques: A handbook for college faculty.* San Francisco, CA: Jossey-Bass.

Berry, E. (2010). The both-and of undergraduate education: Burke's linguistic approach. In P. M. Smudde (Ed.), *Humanistic critique of education: Teaching and learning as symbolic action* (pp. 61–91). West Lafayette, IN: Parlor Press.

Bichelmeyer, B. A. (2005). "The ADDIE model" – A metaphor for the lack of clarity in the field of IDT. *IDT Record*. Retrieved October 4, 2008, from http://www.indiana.edu/~idt/shortpapers/documents/IDTf_Bic.pdf

Bloom, B. S. (Ed.) (1956). *Taxonomy of educational objectives: The classification of educational goals. Book I: Cognitive domain*. New York, NY: Longman.

Brown, A., & Green, T. D. (2011). *The essentials of instructional design: Connecting fundamental principles with process and practice* (2nd ed.). Boston, MA: Pearson.

Fink, L. D. (2013). *Creating significant learning experiences: An integrated approach to designing college courses* (Revised & updated ed.). San Francisco, CA: Jossey-Bass.

Gardiner, L. F. (2005). Research on learning and student development and its implications. In R. M. Diamond & B. Adam (Eds.), *Field guide to academic leadership* (pp. 89–110). San Francisco, CA: Jossey-Bass, John Wiley & Sons.

Gower, K. K. (2008). *Legal and ethical considerations for public relations* (2nd ed.). Long Grove, IL: Waveland Press.

Hubball, H., & Burt, H. (2004). An integrated approach to developing and implementing learning-centered curricula. *International Journal for Academic Development, 9*(1), 51–65.

Kaufman, L. S., & Weiner, S. J. (2015). The CAO and the curriculum: Developing and implementing effective programs for a contemporary student. In J. Martin, J. E. Samels, & Associates (Eds.), *The provost's handbook: The role of the chief academic officer* (pp. 102–110). Baltimore, MD: Johns Hopkins University Press.

Kern-Foxworth, M. (2015). Introducing gender and diversity issues in public relations courses. In B. D. Neff & T. L. Johnson (Eds.), *Learning to teach: What you need to know to develop a successful career as a public relations educator* (4th ed., chapter 2.2). New York, NY: Public Relations Society of America. (Published in electronic form for download or on CD-ROM)

Kuh, G. D., Ikenberry, S. O., Jankowski, N. A., Cain, T. R., Ewell, P. T., Hutchings, P., & Kinzie, J. (Eds.) (2015). *Using evidence of student learning to improve higher education*. San Francisco, CA: Jossey-Bass.

Landis, K. (2019). The public relations industry is too white and the solution starts with higher education. *INSIGHT into Diversity, 93*(1), 52–55.

Lane, A. B., & Johnston, K. A. (2016). *Building bridges: scaffolding the public relations writing curriculum*. Paper presented at the 2016 International Communication Association Convention, in Fukuoka, Japan. Retrieved from EBSCOhost.

Lattuca, L. R., & Stark, J. S. (2009). *Shaping the college curriculum: Academic plans in context* (2nd ed.). San Francisco, CA: Jossey-Bass.

Mackh, B. M. (2018). *Higher education by design: Best practices for curricular planning and instruction*. New York, NY: Routledge.

Molenda, M. (2003). In search of the elusive ADDIE model. *Performance Improvement, 42*(5), 34–35.

Molenda, M. (2004). ADDIE model. In A. Kovalchick & K. Dawson (Eds.), *Educational Technology: An Encyclopedia* (pp. 7–10). Santa Barbara, CA: ABC-CLIO.

Moore, D. T. (2013). *Engaged learning in the academy: Challenges and possibilities*. New York, NY: Palgrave Macmillan.

Neff, B. D., & Johnson, T. L. (Eds.) (2015). *Learning to teach: What you need to know to develop a successful career as a public relations educator* (4th ed.). New York, NY: Public Relations Society of America.

Peterson, C. (2003). Bringing ADDIE to life: Instructional design at its best. *Journal of Educational Multimedia and Hypermedia, 12*(3), 227–241.

Quality Matters (2018). *Higher education rubric workbook: Standards for course design* (6th ed.). Annapolis, MD: Author.

Smudde, P. M. (2023). *Managing public relations: Principles and tools for strategic communication* (2nd ed.). New York, NY: Routledge.

Svinicki, M. D., & McKeachie, W. J. (2014). *McKeachie's teaching tips: Strategies, research, and theory for college and university teachers* (14th ed.). Belmont, CA: Wadsworth, Cengage Learning.

Tsetsura, K. (2011). How understanding multidimensional diversity can benefit global public relations education. *Public Relations Review, 37,* 530–535.

Welty, G. (2007). The "design" phase of the ADDIE model. *Journal of GXP Compliance, 11*(4), 40–52.

Woolard, C. (2017). *Engaging civic engagement: Framing the civic engagement movement in higher education.* Lanham, MD: Lexington Books.

9

ASSESSING LEARNING

This chapter addresses the importance of measuring the effectiveness of teaching and student learning—as a matter as much as for individual students and professors as well as for whole programs. Assessment likely may be mandated. A basic approach to academic assessment is presented as a framework for measuring student learning and the effectiveness of a public relations program and its courses.

An old saying in business is, "You can't manage what you don't measure." The same is true in academia, and assessment measures for student learning are essential. Technically speaking, teachers at all levels have always had to measure their students' learning, but only since 1985, with the First National Conference on Assessment in Higher Education, has assessment of learning become a formal process (Krider, 2015). Note that assessment of student learning is *not* grading. Grading is a mark of a student's achievement against defined performance criteria on any given assignment. Assessment examines the effectiveness of a course's assignments, a whole course, and/or a larger curriculum in a particular discipline measured against defined learning objectives and outcomes so that student learning can be documented and improved. The formal process of academic assessment involves the collection, analysis, reporting, and application of evidence of student learning gained about academic activity in a program of study, from the assignment level to the curriculum level (Angelo, 1999; Bollag, 2006; Brown, Bucklow, & Clark, 2002; McDaniel, 2006). Given the internal and external forces that are at play in the development and sustaining of any academic curriculum (see Chapter 8), the proof that students have

DOI: 10.4324/9781003501817-13

gained the knowledge, skills, and abilities that institutions and their program say they gain is necessary because there is little to no acknowledgment of what they do with what they learn, especially after graduation.

Importance of Assessment

What is unsettling to most faculty is the idea of having to engage in an assessment effort at the operational level that rolls up to the institutional level (see McDaniel, 2006). The connections between what one does in her/his course and one's department are clearer than the connections between one's course and the entire institution. The links, however, are there, and administration and faculty must work together to understand that workability. Figure 9.1 shows an example of the interrelationships among an institution's levels concerning student learning. The administration must help the faculty "connect the dots" about how and why assessment done at operational levels must be aligned and synchronized with institutional-level objectives and goals. Again, we can't manage what we don't measure, and if we don't measure student learning effectively from the classroom to the institution, we can't manage what we do and how we define the value we contribute as educators and institutions.

INSTITUTION
Graduates of this institution will be able to analyze arguments, create and test models, solve problems, evaluate ideas, and verify the reasonableness of conclusions.

DEPARTMENT
Upon completion of the core curriculum, students will be able to be critical consumers and sources of information in verbal and visual media across varied contexts.

COURSE
Upon completion of the course, students will become credible message creators and communication counselors about particular subjects important to their organizations, their leaders, and their constituents.

FIGURE 9.1 Institution- to course-level student learning outcomes (Based on Barkley, E.F. and Major, C.H., *Learning assessment techniques: A handbook for college faculty*, Jossey-Bass, San Francisco, CA, 2016, p. 16.)

An institution's strategic plan is the key, and all operating units have their own ways to fit into that plan that they are responsible to articulate and enact. Assessment as a formal process applies to a program of study's role in institutional success. A general approach to assessment by Allen (2004, p. 10), for example, involves a six-step process:

1. Develop learning objectives.
2. Check for alignment between the curriculum and the objectives.
3. Develop an assessment plan.
4. Collect assessment data.
5. Use results to improve the program.
6. Routinely examine the assessment process and correct, as needed.

This six-step process is a useful framework at an institutional level as it is at a course or program level. In this process, steps one and two must be designed to complement the institution's strategic plan and performance measures like retention, academic performance, etc. Making assessment more a part of the daily business of higher-ed institutions makes it easier to do.

Many books, conference papers, and journal articles address approaches for assessment. That fact is important because we educators must know how to determine how well students are learning what we plan for them to learn. This knowledge about student learning is gained through various methods, such as direct/indirect, authentic, and embedded assessment techniques in courses and programs (see Allen, 2004; Barkley & Major, 2016; Huba & Freed, 2000; Kuh et al., 2015; Maki, 2004; Shavelson, 2010; Walvoord, 2004). Based on that knowledge, if things could be better, educators can and must make adjustments; and if things work well, educators know where to capitalize on success and avoid problems.

For public relations education, specific treatments of assessment are few. Chapter 4 showed guidelines for public relations programs at undergraduate and graduate levels, and those guidelines include references to measuring student learning on selected dimensions. Individual scholarship published about assessment for PRE include measuring student learning through service learning work completed in the traditional campaigns capstone course (Werder & Strand, 2011), through evaluating PR students' value added on the job after completing specific work-related content (Swart, 2014), through a summary treatment of salient assessment matters for PRE (Krider, 2015), and through reflective thinking and feedback about PR gained through a program of study (Mules, 2018). Assessment is very much a collaborative thing, as all faculty (especially in a given program) must work well together to plan, measure, analyze, and improve academic offerings. Assessment also is an individual thing, as each faculty member must be intellectually, attitudinally, and behaviorally committed to knowing what works, why, and how to improve it for one's self, for students, for the program, for the department, and for the institution.

Making Assessment Work

Assessment of student learning and program effectiveness at any scale (from assignment to course to curriculum to institution) is not a one-size-fits-all thing. Because of the factors involved and covered in the preceding chapters, any assessment approach must be custom-made. For example, an institution's overall objectives for student learning and success are part of the context for preparing all aspects of a program of study, and, if they apply, external accreditation standards may apply in the context as well. Additionally and centrally, a curriculum or program of study, such as one for public relations, would articulate vision, mission, learning objectives, program content, data gathering and analysis, and other matters. So, a program's assessment plan (see Appendix E for an example template), which must support the institutional (and accreditation) standards, would be necessary to ensure that individual courses individually and collectively are living up to expectations and open for improvements as needed.

Even so, there are general principles that are highly useful to devise an assessment approach that can be suited to the level(s) to be measured—assignment, course, curriculum, and so on. Although there are multiple approaches (and many are similar but with subtle differences based on their authors' treatments of assessment), Allen's (2004) process approach for developing assessment is a solid, general one for assessing student learning and program effectiveness in public relations education. The process for developing any assessment approach must be collaborative, especially as multiple professors can be assigned to lead multiple sections of a given course, which makes coordinating assessments challenging in larger programs. Following Allen's model, there are six steps.

1. *Develop learning objectives.*

    These statements, as the starting point in any assessment approach, are foundational to all other subsequent matters and activities of assessment, since they are the criteria upon which success in student learning would be measured. Learning objectives (introduced in Chapter 8) at the program level and at the course level are developed and supported among program faculty. At the program level, any course required in it must fulfill one or more program-based learning objectives. Program-based learning objectives are holistic for what students should become by the end of their studies in a curriculum. The following learning objectives come from the PR program at Illinois State:

    • Recall foundational knowledge about the practice, management, value, and history of public relations.
    • Demonstrate competence through application of foundational and specialized knowledge in particular public relations problems and discourse.

- Construct a view of the profession and its future that integrates lessons across all realms of experience about public relations.
- Navigate organizational structures and processes for public relations and beyond.
- Inspire students to care about and value ethical work in a professional setting in every respect and about the general roles of public relations technicians and managers/leaders.
- Introduce resources and strategies for life-long learning about effective and ethical public relations.
- Foster sound skills for effective project management within the public relations process.
- Apply principles/rules for argumentation, discourse, grammar, AP style, and APA style correctly and appropriately in written work.

At the course level, while an individual instructor may take the lead in articulating learning objectives, all program faculty ought to weigh in on the pertinence of a course's learning objectives as both a matter of achieving particular learning objectives among students in and for that course and as a matter of contributing to the fulfillment of the program's learning objectives. An example of course-level learning objectives is given in Appendix B and are listed here:

- Identify characteristics and practices of internal communications in organizations.
- Recall and apply key concepts, terms, and principles for the operations and management of internal communications functions.
- Analyze effective communications functions and recognize "best practices."
- Demonstrate command of the process and use of language by analyzing cases and solving specific communication problems.
- Connect principles and practices about successful communications within this course and across other courses and students' experiences.
- Prepare students for work in a professional setting in terms of how they will be expected to think and act when given internal communications challenges.
- Nurture an attitude of and introduce resources for life-long learning about effective internal communications.

How would you arrive at any learning objective? In the writing of learning objectives, anything reasonable and defensible within the context and purpose of a course or curriculum can be selected and then measured validly and reliably. In this way, as in the two examples above, the best place to start writing any learning objective is to think backwards, with the end in mind—the outcome from student learning through whatever is used, assigned, engaged, and so on. This technique works whether you are devising a lesson, an assignment, a course, or a curriculum. This "backward design" approach, which as Fink (2013) prescribes, focuses on deep processing. For Fink, learning is possible only when change occurs in a learner, and learning involves deep processing such that "significant learning requires that there be some kind of lasting change that is important in terms of the learner's life" (p. 34). The deep processing is possible through six kinds of significant learning, which are shown and defined concisely in Figure 9.2. Each kind of learning works individually and, especially, interactively so that significant learning can be obtained in one or more ways, engaging deep processing of material synergistically through one or more kinds of learning at once. Writing learning objectives, which, in turn, directs how teacher and students engage, needs pertinent verbs that suit each of the six kinds of significant learning (e.g., the lists of verbs about Bloom's taxonomy in Figure 8.2 and available online can help in this regard) so that learning objectives can be articulated clearly, concisely, and concretely.

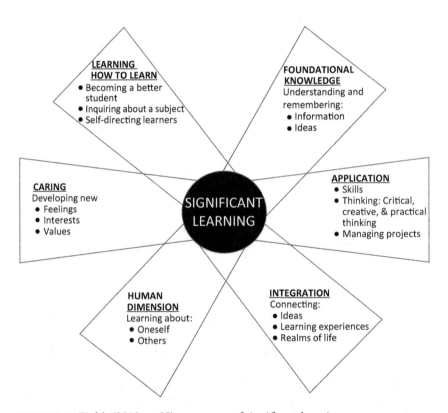

FIGURE 9.2 Fink's (2013, p. 35) taxonomy of significant learning

To illustrate how assessment can be designed, Appendix B contains three documents that matter in assessment for a particular course: a syllabus, an "assessment manual," and a sample assignment. The first part of Appendix B is the syllabus, which includes all the pertinent content mentioned in Chapter 8. In terms of assessment, the syllabus shows learning objectives that are written according to Fink's taxonomy, cross applying verbs for Bloom's taxonomy (Anderson et al., 2001; Bloom, 1956) that fit Fink's taxonomy (see Fink, 2013, p. 34). The first two objectives pertain to foundational knowledge, and each of the rest pertain to each of the remaining kinds of significant learning in Figure 9.2. A diagram of the course's design is given to extend these learning objectives into three particular areas of public relations that matter to the course. Central to the diagram (Fredstrom, 2012) is the dark box that shows a "transformational goal," which is the vision that the learning objectives are to realize for each student. The transformational goal, similar to a "learning outcome," is a vision statement for how a student would be changed when emerging from the course. Tied to that transformational goal are three categories of study that pertain to the course and are defined accordingly. Each category of study ties to multiple learning assessments that are formal (i.e., assigned) and informal (i.e., observed). The assessment manual addresses each of these assessment points, and individual assignments are given separately for formal assessments that enact what is stated for them in the assessment manual. The syllabus, too, summarizes the utility and importance of formal and informal means of assessment.

Also in Appendix B is an assessment manual, which presents the diagram and the definitions of formal and informal assessments that are in the syllabus. Most important, the assessment manual summaries of all the formal and informal points for measuring student learning that support the learning objectives. Each assessment point is structured similarly, stating an assessment point's purpose; the outcome in terms of knowledge, skill, or ability acquired; the input required of the student from one or more kinds of significant learning employed; and the output expected. These summaries guide the creation of individual assignments that are presented in detail separately to students. The manual also helps students grasp the core matters about how their learning develops from the work they do.

The last part of Appendix B includes one example assignment that connects with the assessment manual and the syllabus, and the assignment includes a rubric of the evaluation criteria to measure learning based on the output created that supports the course's learning objectives and reflects on the program's learning objectives. In terms of background on the assignment and why it is used, it is a real-world case that, along with others, was used in class to spur discussion about any given day's concepts, principles, or practices. The assignment is designed to build upon the students' learning experiences throughout the course to culminate in a final product they submit at the end of the semester. The schedule in the syllabus shows when the assignment is given so students could, at the close of each class meeting, write notes and ideas about the day's (and previous days') material that would apply to solving the problem in this case. This case was the only part given to the students without any further information about the assignment. Definitions of key terms about the subject were also given to the students the first day it was assigned. Later on, the full assignment would be given to all students, and they would form teams of four (or so) students to complete the project by its due date at the semester's end. In terms of assessment, the rubric measures how well a student learned and executed on the salient matters of the course that are sought in the assignment because it is a capstone project for the course. In this way, the assignment would be seen to fulfill one or more learning objectives for the course. The assignment itself, when examined for its fit with program learning objectives, would be measured for the degree to which it fulfills one or more program learning objectives.

Depending on how a department or school is organized, a program may have a coordinator who manages all aspects of the program, from leading course design efforts to scheduling of classes. Alternatively, the department/school chair may be the point person for managing the program. And in either case, there likely will be a review process among faculty to decide whether to approve or deny course and program changes. Such a process would be articulated in the unit's policies and procedures documents.

2. *Check for alignment between the curriculum and the objectives.*
With the objectives articulated, the next step is to make sure what is planned to be covered in a course or a curriculum meets those objectives. An easy way to check for alignment between what is offered and what is expected can be done, for example, at the curriculum level (i.e., organizing courses versus program learning objectives) or at the course level (i.e., organizing assignments versus the course's learning objectives). Figure 9.3 shows a very general design for a matrix to determine where and how learning objectives align among a curriculum's courses or among a course's assignments, depending on which level of assessment is the subject. For each course or assignment, a learning objective can be shown simply as addressed or, if more detail is desired, shown for the level of proficiency (i.e., introduced in concept, applied in a form of practice, or demonstrated in problem-based outputs) with a corresponding code for each level.

Course or Assignment	LEARNING OBJECTIVES						
	1	2	3	4	5	6	7
Title 1	X		X		X		
Title 2		X	X				
Title 3			X	X	X		
Title 4					X		X
Title 5	X	X	X		X	X	

FIGURE 9.3 Assessment matrix example (simple approach)

With the matrix in place, the content of individual courses can be accomplished, focusing on in-class and out-of-class work that enables student learning in tune with one or more learning objectives. The assessment manual in Appendix B is one way of making such connections during course planning and implementation. All along the way, linkages to support services for student learning, facilities, technologies, and other matters can be identified and applied. Additionally, particular aspects about teaching methods, grading approaches, and other relevant matters can be discussed among faculty to make improvements based on their shared experiences leading courses.

3. *Develop an assessment plan.*

Whether the subject of focus is one course or a whole curriculum/program, a plan to assess its effectiveness—its successfulness in fulfilling learning objectives—is needed. Example assessment plans can be found Appendix E presents an example assessment plan. You may find other such templates easily enough on the Internet. The framework for an assessment plan can be whatever works within the context of the institution's requirements, accreditation standards, and program vision and mission. Indeed, the most basic contents for an assessment plan are vision, mission, learning objectives, program content, data gathering and analysis, and other necessary matters. Again see Appendix E for an example to get you started.

The crux of an assessment plan is to articulate how pertinent data about student learning and program effectiveness at any level will be gathered and, then, analyzed. From individual samples of students' completed assignments in courses, to focus groups of alumni, to surveys of employers of program graduates, to analyses of competing institutions' programs, the data can be anything that is reasonable and defensible, plus the methodology must be valid (i.e., measure only what is supposed to be measured) and reliable (i.e., measures what is supposed to be measured every time). If your institution has a unit that is focused on assessment, it would be best to work with it from the outset, as that unit will know well what the requirements are and the "best practices" that can help you. The experts in this unit or other appropriate unit, such as institutional research, would also provide guidance about any ethical and legal matters that may be necessary to address, such as if the data and findings gained through human subjects was to be published in some way. As long as data are used solely in any effort to improve an academic program, the work is exempt from institutional review for involving human subjects.

4. *Collect assessment data.*

The assessment data come from two kinds of measurements: direct and indirect assessments of student learning. These measurements taken at the course and student levels are necessary for measuring program effectiveness as well. There are various ways to apply these assessments of student learning (in synch with standards for public relations education; see Chapter 4), with direct assessment being the most essential.

Data gathered from *direct assessments* of students' work come from tangible evidence of what students have and have not learned (see "Assessment Manual" in Appendix B). Methods for direct assessment include tests and quizzes, comprehensive exams, oral exams, interviews, papers, projects, case analyses, performances, exhibitions, and portfolios. These direct assessments at the course and student levels ("microlevel") would reveal the following evidence that course objectives are met; prerequisite knowledge, skills, and abilities (KSAs) are retained and applied from prior coursework; foundational knowledge is covered and applied; areas for continuous improvement are identified and addressed (strengths, weaknesses, recommendations); and assignments cultivate many/most KSAs that are necessary and sufficient for new professionals (see Chapter 4 for standards for PRE and, if they apply, accreditation standards). The use of rubrics in direct assessments (see example assignment in Appendix B) would be instrumental in codifying the criteria on which students' work would be evaluated within the specific context of given assignments and within the broader context of an overall course and its learning objectives. Faculty would need to retain copies of all rubrics for all students' assignments (i.e., digital copies preferred) so that data about student performance can be used to drill down into what works and what doesn't work in courses and the PR program by tracking performance over time, at least in terms of standards for PRE presented in Chapter 4.

Data gathered from *indirect assessments* of student learning (see "Assessment Manual" in Appendix B) are "proxy signs" outside of course-based assignments that show students probably learned content, especially through the reference points in standards given in Chapter 4. Methods for indirect assessment include student and alumni surveys, interviews, focus groups, and reflective essays; feedback about interns' performance (also can serve as direct evidence when coupled with a specific performance rubric); program reputation and quality; selected items from faculty course evaluations; retention and graduation rates; job placements; career advancements; honors and awards; and anecdotal information from individuals related to the program in any way. Depending on a course's design and learning objectives, certain stakeholders would serve as assessors of student learning through direct and indirect measures of students' work, and those assessors can be faculty (of course the class instructor), students, class clients (i.e., in service learning context), internship/field experience supervisors, alumni, and employers of graduates.

5. *Use results to improve the program.*

   With all the data collected and sorted, now is the time to make them make sense and add value by improving things where possible. So, this fifth step is all about data analysis and reporting. The best mindset for this step is simplicity in the approach and temper it with effectiveness in examining what is being measured and directness in drawing inferences and making recommendations. The ultimate goal in this step is to make complex information about student learning and program effectiveness—all of which reflect back on the pertinent learning objectives—meaningful in concise, concrete, and compelling ways. An important concern in this step is deciding in advance how any outcomes (especially negative ones) would be addressed so there is not a personal attack on anyone.

   Data for analysis come from the sources used in the previous step in the assessment process. Depending on the methods used for gathering data, multiple assessment techniques are permissible that illuminate what the data mean in comparison to the learning objective(s) they measure. Examples of such data-analysis techniques are content analyses of verbal data gained in surveys, interviews, and focus groups; and another is scoring rubrics about whether or how well course content fulfills stated learning objectives.

   Any approach for coding data (called a "coding scheme") ought to be tested before it is employed. Such a "pilot test" involves, for example, people working in teams of two or three to discuss a sample of data with the coding scheme to arrive at consensus about findings from the sample. Any discrepancies that team members have can be remedied through discussion about problems and agreement on solutions, resulting in any adjustments in the coding scheme for when it is actually used to analyze data. In such data-analysis techniques, the reliability of the people coding the data must be measured. The reason is that subjective judgments are made based on stated criteria (i.e., learning objectives), which are the substance of the data analysis. So, the pilot test functions to determine inter-rater reliability (IRR) to demonstrate whether there is a high degree of consistency (i.e., what is being measured is measured each time by whomever is involved) in everyone's use of the analysis method on the dataset being analyzed.

Very simply, IRR can be determined by having coders rate a small sample of data with the pertinent coding scheme. The number of times coders gave identical ratings in a sample of data is compared to the number of times they gave differing ratings by, say, one point and by two points and so on, depending on the rating scale. A simple calculation for IRR is based on the coders' agreements versus disagreements (see Statistics How To, 2019), and the result is a percentage, the closer it is to 1.0 (perfect agreement) the better, with any IRR score in the .90s indicating high reliability. (Depending on the kind of data used and the number of coders, a more complex calculation, like Cohen's Kappa, can be used instead.) If the IRR is not satisfactory, the method needs some correction to the coding scheme to remove the inconsistencies between coders, then coders need to be retrained, and the scheme needs to be retested, making changes in the scheme as needed. Once IRR is shown to be satisfactory and the method for applying the coding scheme is robust, the full analysis of all data can begin.

With the data analyzed, a report on the findings is needed. Such a report should be simple and direct, summarizing the assessment's purpose(s) in the context of the assessment plan, method(s) in obtaining data, approach(es) for analyzing data, and findings, recommendations for action, and any outcomes obtained from implementing recommendations. The master organizational approach for the report's section about findings, recommendations, and outcomes should be the learning objectives that pertain to the level at which the assessment was conducted (i.e., assignment, course, or curriculum/program). Explanations about what data were collected and used for each learning objective put the findings in context so that meaningful inferences can be drawn that support sound recommendations for corrective action, if such action is needed. Again, great care should be taken in advance in being ready to handle negative outcomes/findings so that the possibility of personal attacks is eliminated and the greater good for students and the program is addressed.

6. *Routinely examine the assessment process and correct it, as needed.*
   Continuous improvement is a key concept in education as much as in industry. Having an assessment plan and using it well matter. From individual instructors to program faculty to department/school leaders, to university administration, there must be a positive and supportive environment and infrastructure for assessment. Programs for orientation to and training in assessment of student learning are essential so that anyone who wants and needs to measure the effectiveness of programs, courses, and assignments can do it well. Assessment, then, should be routine, as instructors collect needed data that suit their assessment plans and, most important, discuss what they see and prepare for the next periodic round of formal analysis and reporting of assessment data. Overall, the point to assessment is to

ensure student learning results on the order of the stated learning objectives related to assignments, courses, and programs. Stagnation and complacency are not options! As factors change in a field—much like communication technology changes affect the work of public relations professionals—the purposes, content, and approaches to educating students can change and be measured for effectiveness through a revised assessment plan. And so the cycle continues.

A Question for You

What are your feelings about and expectations for assessing students' learning?

In my experience, the complexity of academic assessment is like anything else of such importance, and it becomes internalized over time. I found early on that many faculty detest assessment because they see it as a major interruption to what they were hired to do—teach, produce scholarship or creative works, and serve the greater good on and off campus. Plus many believe what they do is enough for their classes, and the whole idea of academic assessment is (at best) window dressing and (at worst) some dastardly effort to find out who is not working hard enough so programs and their respective personnel can be cut. The lure of conspiracy theories exists in academia too. To me, having come from industry, I could understand the impetus for such negative attitudes but disavow them for a more prudent perspective about why assessment matters, for example, from the micro level (individual students and faculty) to the macro levels (alumni success and institutional reputation).

The raw idea of measuring student learning and the effectiveness of assignments, courses, and programs/curricula was intriguing to me because it paralleled what I knew from industry, but I had never thought of that before becoming a full-time academic. Participating in workshops about, reading sources on, and designing and working through academic assessments was highly valuable. The importance for truly knowing how good something is and demonstrating that goodness to others is very important, especially to outside constituents. Outsiders to academia tend to think they know what goes on in colleges and universities, operating on vague assumptions as if they are truths of the reality of higher education. (Recall the content of Chapter 3.) Even insiders to our own institutions can assume too much, if they choose to live by assumptions alone.

The upshot, then, is that assessment of student learning and program/curriculum effectiveness results in tangible, meaningful, actionable, and compelling demonstrations of what educators and students do *together* that results in significant learning and, thereby, added value to society. Assessment also shows how we can become better and stronger and with what resources to help us get there, thereby being essential to the business case for whatever is needed. So, assessment is just as much an educational effort as anything else teachers do. As long as professors are the ones who are enabling student learning, their work in demonstrating that outcome is essential.

References

Allen, M. J. (2004). *Assessing academic programs in higher education.* Bolton, MA: Anker Publishing.

Anderson, L. W., Krathwohl, D. R., Airasian, P. W., Cruikshank, K. A., Mayer, R. E., Pintrich, P. R., Raths, J., & Wittrock, M. C. (Eds.) (2001). *A taxonomy of learning, teaching, and assessing: A revision of Bloom's taxonomy of educational objectives* (Complete ed.). New York: Longman.

Angelo, T. A. (1999). Doing assessment as if learning matters most. *AAHE Bulletin, 51*(9), 3–6.

Barkley, E. F., & Major, C. H. (2016). *Learning assessment techniques: A handbook for college faculty.* San Francisco, CA: Jossey-Bass.

Bloom, B. S. (Ed.) (1956). *Taxonomy of educational objectives: The classification of educational goals. Book I: Cognitive domain.* New York: Longman.

Bollag, B. (2006, October 27). Making an art form of assessment. *Chronicle of Higher Education, 53*(10), A8–A10.

Brown, S., Bucklow, C., & Clark, P. (2002). Professionalizing teaching: Enhancing the status of teaching, improving the experience of learning and supporting innovation in higher education. *Journal of Geography in Higher Education, 26*(2), 159–168.

Fink, L. D. (2013). *Creating significant learning experiences: An integrated approach to designing college courses* (revised & updated ed.). San Francisco, CA: Jossey-Bass.

Fredstrom, T. (2012). *Reinvent your course.* Normal, IL: Illinois State University.

Huba, M. E., & Freed, J. E. (2000). *Learner-centered assessment on college campuses.* Boston, MA: Allyn & Bacon.

Krider, D. S. (2015). Assessing public relations education. In B. D. Neff & T. L. Johnson (Eds.), *Learning to teach: What you need to know to develop a successful career as a public relations educator* (4th ed., pp. 246–258). New York, NY: Public Relations Society of America.

Kuh, G. D., Ikenberry, S. O., Jankowski, N. A., Cain, T. R., Ewell, P. T., Hutchings, P., & Kinzie, J. (Eds.) (2015). *Using evidence of student learning to improve higher education.* San Francisco, CA: Jossey-Bass.

Maki, P. L. (2004). *Assessing for learning: Building a sustainable commitment across the institution.* Sterling, VA: Stylus.

McDaniel, T. R. (2006). "Assessmania" and "bureaupathology" in higher education. *Academic Leader, 22*(6), 8, 7.

Mules, P. (2018). Reflection on the absence of formal reflection in public relations education and practice. *Public Relations Review, 44*, 174–179.

Shavelson, R. J. (2010). *Measuring college learning responsibly: Accountability in a new era.* Stanford, CA: Stanford University Press.

Statistics How To. (2019). *Inter-rater reliability IRR: Definition, calculation.* Retrieved from https://www.statisticshowto.datasciencecentral.com/inter-rater-reliability/

Swart, C. (2014). An assessment of work-integrated learning or public relations in an open distance learning context. *Public Relations Review, 40,* 387–396.

Walvoord, B. E. (2004). *Assessment clear and simple: A practical guide for institutions, departments, and general education.* San Francisco, CA: Jossey-Bass.

Werder, K. P., & Strand, K. (2011). Measuring student outcomes: An assessment of service-learning in the public relations campaigns course. *Public Relations Review, 37,* 478–484.

APPENDIX A: PRETENURE PERFORMANCE TRACKING TOOL

New faculty very often would like to have some kind of guidance for what they need to produce in the three areas of academia of teaching, research, and service.

This file is one that I designed for that purpose that can be used informally (i.e., for and by one's self to track progress in each of the three areas, which can be handy for working with a mentor too) or formally (i.e., in consultation with a department/school's committee responsible for personnel-performance reviews that matter for reappointment, promotion, and tenure). Either way, this form is meant to provide a structure to what can seem like nebulous pursuits as an educator and scholar.

The form is divided into three sections, one for each of the three academic areas that are considered for reappointment, promotion, and tenure. Footnotes are placed in certain places (and defined on the last page) to clarify content requirements. The rows in each section present a thorough but not exhaustive list of the products that would pertain in their respective academic areas. It's possible that certain products would not be considered or relevant in one's position in a department/school. If that case is true, don't worry about that row/ line item. In fact, this file can and should be customized so that it fits the needs of a person and a department/school.

The "Year" columns can be used as is for check or tally marks to show very simply how many products in a line item have been produced in a given year. Alternatively, the file could be reoriented to a landscape layout so the "Year" columns could be widened to add more detail as desired.

Recording the dates of "Pretenure Meeting Dates" with mentors or personnel-review committees is important to show so you can ensure that your progress has been discussed and any counsel given is retained.

Faculty Name: _____

Semester & Year Joined Faculty: _____

Number of Years Credited, if any: _____

Pretenure Meeting Dates:
_____
_____
_____
_____

Teaching Performance	Year 1	Year 2	Year 3	Year 4	Year 5
Annual letter assessment[1]					
Courses developed					
Programs developed					
Program assessment plans developed & approved					
Textbooks published					
SoTL contributions					
Thesis/Dissertation committees (chair & member)					
Independent study/research supervision					
Internship supervision (graduate)					
Teaching award					
Professional development					

Research/Creative Works Produced[2]	Year 1	Year 2	Year 3	Year 4	Year 5
Annual letter assessment[1]					
Public presentation of creative work (peer reviewed)					
Public presentation of creative work (no peer review)					
Peer-reviewed journal articles					
Invited journal articles					
Peer-reviewed book chapters					
Invited book chapters					
Books written					
Books edited					
Peer-reviewed conference papers					
Conference panels (chair/participant/respondent)					
Conference posters					
Conference proceedings					
Major or keynote speech					
Published mass-media periodical piece					
Invited pieces and encyclopedia entries					
Interview by news/media outlet for produced story					
External grants applied/granted					
Internal grants applied/granted					
Awards					

Service Contributions	Year 1	Year 2	Year 3	Year 4	Year 5
Annual letter assessment[1]					
Manuscript reviews (conf/jnl/bk)/Creative work judging					
School/Department					
College					
University					
Discipline					
Community					

[1] Note: Annual performance categories are evaluated annually against established criteria in the academic unit (consistent with institutional requirements for reappointment, promotion, and tenure) and given a rating that asserts the level of performance from highest/best to lowest/worst, such as outstanding, very good, satisfactory, poor/unsatisfactory. Such levels also can be indicated by numerical scores or another approach.

[2] A categorization of research and creative work (categories and their contents are presented in a traditional order of importance but can be reordered as needed):

Peer-Reviewed Product
- Journal Article or Public Presentation of Creative Work
- Book Chapter
- Conference Paper

Substantial Product
- Authored Book or Public Presentation of Creative Work
- Edited Book
- External Grant
- Internal Grant
- Major/Keynote Speech
- Original Work Included in Conference Proceedings

Significant Product
- Invited Book Chapter
- Invited Journal Article
- Published Mass-media Periodical Piece
- Conference Panel
- Conference Poster
- Journal Manuscript Review
- Book Manuscript Review
- Conference Paper Review
- Judge of Creative Products
- Interview by News/Media Outlet
- Invited Piece (Other Academic or Nonacademic Outlet)
- Encyclopedia Entry

APPENDIX B: EXAMPLE COURSE-MANAGEMENT DOCUMENTS

This appendix presents selected documents that can help in designing and assessing assignments, courses, or curricula. A companion website for this book would have the documents here and others for download.

COM 373 INTERNAL PUBLIC RELATIONS

School of Communication

Illinois State University

Fall Semester

Class Meetings:	TT 3:35-4:50 in Fell 148
Lead Student:	Peter M. Smudde, PhD, APR
Office:	449 Fell Hall
Office Hours:	M-Th 1-3 and by appointment
Office Phone:	(309) 438-7339
E-mail:	psmudde@ilstu.edu

Catalog Course Description

Principles and practices for communicating with organizations' internal audiences. Investigation includes nonprofit, profit, government, and non-government organizations. Can be taken for graduate credit. Prerequisites: COM 111; COM 229 strongly recommended.

(Continued)

Course's Specific Focus

This course is an elective for public relations majors and, for graduate students, can be taken for graduate credit. The course is focused on internal communications, which follows accepted practices in public relations for communicating with organizational members, employees, retirees, and others deemed "internal" or members of an organization's "family." In this way, we also explore globalization communication within organizations' communities. Accordingly, this course will examine the purposes, processes, and products of internal communications efforts within many types of organizations, including companies/corporations, nonprofits, non-governmental organizations, and so on. Theory and practice from the interrelated fields of public relations, human resources, and organizational communication will be bridged through class discussions, readings, and assignments. Course material will be managed largely through ReggieNet and linked with Web-based resources.

Learning Objectives

1. Identify characteristics and practices of internal communications in organizations.
2. Recall and apply key concepts, terms and principles for the operations and management of internal communications functions.
3. Analyze effective communications functions and recognize "best practices."
4. Demonstrate command of the process and use of language by analyzing cases and solving specific communication problems.
5. Connect principles and practices about successful communications within this course, across other courses and students' experiences.
6. Prepare students for work in a professional setting in terms of how they will be expected to think and act when given internal communications challenges.
7. Nurture an attitude of and introduce resources for life-long learning about effective internal communications.

These learning objectives will be fulfilled by focusing on three dimensions of internal public relations (iPR): operations understanding, strategic planning, and professionalism. The combination of these dimensions and the realization of learning objectives will result in one transformational goal for the course. To meet the course's transformational goal,

(Continued)

work in the three dimensions (shown in the ovals in the diagram below) has its own series of assessments of your learning. Each of the three dimensions involves measuring your learning in various ways, some of which are used in more than one dimension. Specific instructions about each assignment are given separately in ReggieNet, and any additional guidance shall be given in class and individually as needed. (See the "Learning Assessments" section below.) The following diagram shows how the dimensions (and their associated learning objectives) lead into the transformational goal.

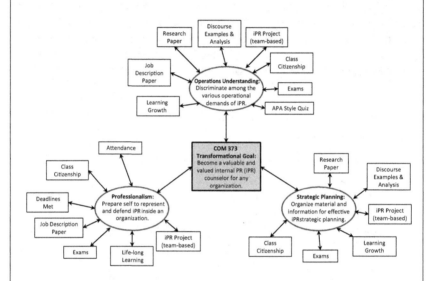

Continued Enrollment

Your enrollment in this class constitutes agreement with all aspects of this syllabus and any additions or alterations that may be made to it during the course of the semester. Additions and alterations include announcements I post for the class in ReggieNet or announce in class, and additions and alternations include e-mail sent to class members. Such additions and alterations include information about the course, assignments, and so on. These announcements and e-mail are equally important when it comes to evaluating your work because announcements may contain clarifications or other help that fit within assignments' requirements.

(*Continued*)

Required Texts

- American Psychological Association. (2009). *Publication manual of the American Psychological Association* (6th ed.). Washington, DC: Author. [NOTE: Purchase the second or later printing]
- Associated Press. (2011). *The Associated Press stylebook and briefing on media law.* New York, NY: Author. [Also available as an iPhone/iPad app.]
- D'Aprix, R. (2009). *The credible company: Communicating with today's skeptical workforce.* San Francisco, CA: Jossey-Bass.
- Quirke, B. (2008). *Making the connections: Using internal communication to turn strategy into action* (2nd ed.). Burlington, VT: Gower.

Required Readings (accessible through ReggieNet)

- Berger, B. K. (2011, October 11). *Employee communication: Let's move from knowing to doing.* The 2011 Grunig Lecture given at the PRSA International Conference, Orlando, FL. [manuscript]
- Burton, K., Grates, G., & Learch, C. (2013). *Best-in-class practices in employee communication: Through the lens of 10 global leaders.* Gainesville, FL: Institute for Public Relations. Retrieved from http://www.institute-forpr.org/best-in-class-practices-in-employee-communication/
- Clampitt, P. G. (2010). Scrutinizing ethical issues. In P. G. Clampitt (Ed.), *Communicating for managerial effectiveness: Problems, strategies, solutions* (4th ed., pp. 45–70). Los Angeles, CA: Sage.
- Heyman Associates (2006, December). New technology primer. *Positioning.* New York, NY: Author. Retrieved from http://heymanassociates.com/sites/heyman/files/themes/files/web/images/Positioning_Dec2006.pdf
- Holtz, S. (2004). Types of employee communications. In S. Holtz (Ed.), *Corporate conversations: A guide to crafting effective and appropriate internal communications* (pp. 35–53). New York, NY: AMACOM.
- Jensen, B. (1995, August). Are we necessary? The case for dismantling corporate communication. *Communication World,* 14–18, 30.
- Morris, T., & Goldsworthy, S. (2008). Internal communications: A case of PR or propaganda? In T. Morris & S. Goldsworthy (Eds.), *PR: A persuasive industry?: Spin, public relations, and the shaping of the modern media* (pp. 129–135). New York, NY: Palgrave Macmillan
- Nevill, C. (2011). New values for a new workplace. In T. L. Gillis (Ed.), *The IABC handbook of organizational communication: A guide to internal communication, public relations, marketing, and leadership* (2nd ed., pp. 471–478). San Francisco, CA: Jossey-Bass.

(Continued)

- Parkinson, M. G., Ekachai, D., & Hetherington, L. T. (2001). Public relations law. In R. L. Heath & G. Vasquez (Eds.), *Handbook of public relations* (pp. 247–257). Thousand Oaks, CA: Sage Publications.
- Ruck, K., & Welch, M. (2012). Valuing internal communication: Management and employee perspectives. *Public Relations Review, 38*, 294–302.
- Smudde, P. M., & Courtright, J. L. (2010). Public relations and power. In R. L. Heath (Ed.), *Handbook of public relations* (2nd ed., pp. 177–189). Thousand Oaks, CA: Sage.
- Smudde, P. M., & Courtright, J. L. (2012). A foreword about "generic" public relations. In P. M. Smudde & J. L. Courtright (Eds.), *Inspiring cooperation & celebrating organizations: Genres, message design & strategy in public relations* (pp. 1–14). New York, NY: Hampton Press.
- Smudde, P. M., & Courtright, J. L. (2012). Framework: Reasons for a generic perspective. In P. M. Smudde & J. L. Courtright (Eds.), *Inspiring cooperation & celebrating organizations: Genres, message design & strategy in public relations* (pp. 15–38). New York, NY: Hampton Press.
- Smudde, P. M., & Courtright, J. L. (2012). Appendix: Families of public relations discourse genres. In P. M. Smudde & J. L. Courtright (Eds.), *Inspiring cooperation & celebrating organizations: Genres, message design & strategy in public relations* (pp. 219–220). New York, NY: Hampton Press.
- Whitworth, B. (2011). Internal communication. In T. L. Gillis (Ed.), *The IABC handbook of organizational communication: A guide to internal communication, public relations, marketing, and leadership* (2nd ed., pp. 195–206). San Francisco, CA: Jossey-Bass.
- Woodall, K. (2011). The future of business communication. In T. L. Gillis (Ed.), *The IABC handbook of organizational communication: A guide to internal communication, public relations, marketing, and leadership* (2nd ed., pp. 514–529). San Francisco, CA: Jossey-Bass.

Outside Preparation

Plan on spending between six to nine hours (or more, depending on how you learn) each week outside of class on your work for this course. (See ISU's Credit Hour Policy 4.1.19. Also see "Time Management/Credit Hour Policy" for weekly and daily breakdown.) You will need this time to complete assigned readings, prepare for class, write papers, develop team projects, and study for exams. You are expected to read, think critically about, and prepare three to five comments or questions about the material before coming to each class meeting. See my "Welcome" note in ReggieNet.

(Continued)

Learning Assessments

Assessment of students' learning against the course's objectives shall be done through a combination of learning assessments:

- Informal/Ungraded Assessments—I can measure how well you are learning *in process* by observing, listening to, and talking with you. These data reveal your personal processes, attitudes, and other matters that are part of how and how well you learn. Examples include chatting about course material before and during class, the quality of questions and discussion in class, the amount of sharing/disclosure, learning ownership, assignment discussion, visits with me, and attitude.
- Formal/Graded Assessments—I can measure how well you can apply your learning by evaluating the *work you produce* in response to specific assignments. This work is what is graded and used to determine your final, overall level of mastery of the course's material by course's end. Graded assessments will be presented separately but summarized below. They also are listed in the grading policy.
  - ✓ *APA Style Quiz*: One 50-point quiz of 25 questions; take-home; open book.
  - ✓ *Papers*: One 100-point and one 200-point paper will be assigned in this course. They are due on the dates shown in the "Course Schedule." You must apply critical thinking skills about the concepts covered in this course to specifically and thoroughly address the problems given in the assignments. The papers will be assigned separately in class. I encourage you to visit with me early and often to make sure you're "on track" with the papers. Research papers must conform to APA style as stated above.
  - ✓ *iPR Discourse Examples*: You will collect a number of real-world, different, and individual examples of internal public relations (iPR) discourse for use in class. The examples will be due on the date in the course schedule when we cover "Discourse approach to iPR." The collection of examples will be scored based on several factors that will be explained separately in the formal assignment.
  - ✓ *iPR Project*: You will work in small teams on an internal public relations project worth 200 points. The project will entail research and

(Continued)

problem-solving analysis that will lead to the formulation of a sound iPR solution, featuring "real-world" business writing components. This project will be assigned separately in class. As with anything in the class, I encourage you to visit with me early and often to make sure you're "on track."

✓ *Exams*: Two 50-question, 100-point exams will be given—one at midterm and one during finals week. The exams will cover selected material from the readings and class meetings up to their respective points in the semester and are designed to assess your learning in terms of your recall of concepts and their application. The exams will have multiple-choice and true-false items. Exam items will feature short scenarios that require you to think critically about what's going on and how to approach communications opportunities as a project leader or department/agency manager.

Graduate Students

In addition to the assignments listed in the "Learning Assessments" section, graduate students will develop a research project germane to the content of this course and suitable for submission to an academic convention. I must approve topics. Details are given separately on ReggieNet, and the basic assignment includes three parts that will be graded individually: a written proposal (2–3 pages), literature review (6–7 pages), and final paper (17–19 pages), which are due at different points in the semester (i.e., each third of the semester), and the student will work with me to determine due dates.

Course Grading Policy

Final grades are assigned on the basis of accumulation of points compared to the set scale below, not percentages. I do not "curve" grades on any assignment or exam, nor do I "curve" final course grades. I evaluate the end products of your work, not effort. Students are encouraged to keep track of the points they have accumulated, and your grades will be posted on ReggieNet so you can monitor your performance, which I encourage you to do frequently. If I make an error in grading, I'll always apologize and make

(Continued)

things right. Here is a breakdown of the point values for the assignments in this course:

Assignment	Available points	Earned points
APA Quiz	50	
iPR Jobs Survey Paper	100	
Research Paper	200	
iPR Discourse Examples	50	
iPR Project	200	
Exam #1	100	
Exam #2	100	
GRADUATE STUDENTS:		
Project Proposal	50	
Lit Review	100	
Final Product	200	
High-tech Device Violations	0 (–5 ea.)	
Perfect Attendance Bonus	20	
Total Points U'grads	800	
Total Points Grads	1,150	

I will reveal scores in the ReggieNet grade book only after I return the graded assignments. If you disagree with my evaluation of your work, please see me during office hours within one week after I have returned your work. I will not discuss grades at any other time thereafter.

I do not "round up" or "round down" points toward final course grades, except in cases for fractions of points, and at that rate, I use conventional rounding procedures, e.g., 839.5 could be rounded to 840, but 839.3 would be rounded to 839. The following scale will be used to determine final grades for **undergraduate students**:

A = 728–800   B = 648–727   C = 568–647   D = 488–567   F = 0–487

The following scale will be used to determine final grades for **graduate students**:

A = 1047–1150   B = 932–1046   C = 817–931   D = 702–816   F = 0–701

For both scales note that the lowest "A" was calculated at 91% of the total possible points and rounded up, the lowest "B" at 81% and rounded up, and

(Continued)

so on. I reserve the right to revise all or part of this grading scale, and any revisions would be announced in class. You are responsible for obtaining any such revisions.

If the calculation for your final grade is within 0.02 points of the next-highest grade, I will consider lifting your final letter grade to the next letter, if and only if your scores on all assignments since the beginning of the semester have consistently improved. If you earned a grade of "F" on any assignment at any time in the semester, this policy will not be applied.

Incompletes will be granted only when a documented emergency prevents you from completing the class, you contacted the Dean of Students Office, and you have successfully completed at least approximately two-thirds (66%) of the course's assignments.

Special Needs

Any student needing to arrange a reasonable accommodation for a documented disability should contact Disability Concerns, Fell 350, 438-5853 (voice), 438-8620 (TDD).

Course Outline   [R] = ReggieNet

Date	Topics & assignments	Readings & assignments due
8/23	Introduction to course. "Learning to learn."	Visit ReggieNet. Print & read syllabus. Get books.
8/25	APA style, research papers & English usage. *Assign APA quiz*	APA manual familiarity. "Essential Skills for PR Majors" (in-class Q&A)
8/30	What is internal PR? *Assign job description paper*	Whitworth [R]. D'Aprix prologue & ch. 1
9/1	What is internal PR's value to organizations? *Give out iPR project case only for note-taking.*	**APA quiz due.** Jensen [R]; Quirke ch. 1.
9/6	Role & Approaches of Persuasion (HHH)	"Persuasion Campaign Models" [R]
9/8	What are ethical, legal & power dimensions?	Clampitt [R]; Parkinson et al. [R]; Smudde & Courtright (2010) [R]
9/13	How does internal PR fit strategically? Writing Objectives, Strategies & Tactics. *Assign research paper*	Quirke ch. 2; "IPR Best In Class" [R]

(Continued)

Date	Topics & assignments	Readings & assignments due
9/15	D'Aprix's INFORMS model for internal PR	D'Aprix ch 2–3
9/20	D'Aprix's INFORMS model for internal PR	**Job description paper due.** D'Aprix ch 4–5
9/22	D'Aprix's INFORMS model for internal PR	D'Aprix ch 6–7
	ME study guide. *Assign iPR discourse examples.*	
9/27	Personal meetings on paper (by appointment)	Draft paper
9/29	Personal meetings on paper (by appointment)	Draft paper
10/4	D'Aprix's INFORMS model for internal PR	D'Aprix ch 8 & Epilogue; Ruck & Welch [R]
	Exam Prep Discussion	
10/6	*Guest Speaker: Jennifer Detweiler*	
10/11	Discourse approach to internal PR, including class exercise on discourse types and uses.	**Research paper due.** Smudde & Courtright (2012) [R]; Holtz (2004) [R]; Heyman Associates (2006) [R]
10/13		**Midterm Exam (8/30–10/4)**
10/18	Midterm Exam Redemption	Bring all course material
10/20	Going global & restructuring. *Assign the rest of the iPR project.*	Quirke ch 3
10/25	Leading engagement	Quirke ch 4
10/27	Making change happen	**iPR discourse examples due.** Quirke ch 5
11/1	*Guest Speaker: Rachel Moore*	Burton, Grates & Learch [R]
11/3	Business Writing. FE study guide.	"Business Writing Truths" [R]; "Elements of Business Writing" [R]; "Seven Cs of Effective Communication" [R]; Quirke ch. 4.
11/8	Personal meetings on iPR project (by appointment)	
11/10	Personal meetings on iPR project (by appointment)	
11/15	Engaging employees face-to-face	Quirke ch 6
11/17	Communication initiatives/ projects &	Quirke ch 7
11/21–25	**Thanksgiving Holiday Break**	
11/29	Planning and managing communication	Quirke ch 8

(Continued)

Date	Topics & assignments	Readings & assignments due
12/1	Repositioning the role of internal PR	Quirke ch 9; Berger [R]
12/6	Measuring impact	**iPR project due.** Quirke ch 10; Ruck & Welch [R]
12/8	Future of internal PR	Morris & Goldsworthy [R];
	Exam Prep Discussion	Nevill [R]; Woodall [R]
12/13		**Final Exam (7:50–9:50 a.m.)**

NOTE: We may alter this course schedule and other aspects of this syllabus as the course progresses. You are responsible for noting any such changes, which will be announced in class and/or posted on ReggieNet.

COURSE POLICIES

In this course, I challenge you to *strive for perfection* (or at least near perfection) in your work. Why? The answer is that your bosses, peers, and, especially, clients will expect that from you throughout your career. So, this course, like the others you've taken, is designed to extend your knowledge, strengthen your analytical skills, and refine your work habits. This course, then, challenges you to think, work, and produce discourse that would rival that of full-time professionals. To manage matters in this course, the several policy areas given below.

Class Civility

The following 12 points are habits that, should you choose to employ them, can help you become successful in this course and contribute to a great learning environment for all of us. The 12 points are not individually or collectively any kind of guarantee about grades you may earn for the course. They make up a prescription for you to effectively manage your work and learn the material in this course.

1. Read, take notes on, develop comments and questions about, and seriously think about the assigned readings before coming to class.
2. Print the appropriate PowerPoint slides (multiple slides per sheet) for note taking—what we say between the lines and graphics is more meaningful. And truly use the relevant resources on ReggieNet prior to attending class. It's also okay to do additional reading and research!

(Continued)

3. Complete assignments/activities to prepare for class.
4. Arrive on-time and attend all classes.
5. Offer helpful comments during discussions and activities and encourage comments from your fellow classmates.
6. Treat everyone with respect.
7. Participate in course activities with enthusiasm and interest. Attitude is key.
8. Be attentive while others are talking or presenting.
9. Only engage in class activities during class.
10. Ensure all electronic devices are turned off during class.
11. Take good notes during class meetings.
12. Visit with me, work with each other, and seek help from students who've taken the class before to learn the material outside of class.

You also are expected to be familiar with ISU's Code of Student Conduct. Concerning online course content, you also are expected to be familiar with and apply principles of Communication/Netiquette.

Cell Phones, Laptops, and Other Devices

Very recent research shows that taking notes by hand with pen/pencil and paper results in far better learning than when taking notes on a digital devise. Even so, you may bring and use a laptop or tablet computer with wireless connectivity during class, but please use it only to help you in your learning this class' content and not surf the Web, check e-mail, or do any other non-class-related stuff. If you find something useful, please share it with the class. Turn off the volume, and no ear phones are allowed.

Please turn **off** all other electronic devices while attending class. *If your phone or pager goes off in class, or if you are using a high-tech device that I have not approved for use in this class, you will automatically lose 5 points for each occurrence.* See me before class if you must have your cell phone on because of a legitimate need to do so. You may use a device only with my approval.

Class Format

We all are students. This class bridges theory and practice, and it relies heavily on discussion and your participation. Topics and appropriate readings are planned for each meeting, and we may pursue other avenues in our

(Continued)

investigation of public relations. *You are expected to read and think critically about the material for each class, which will be important to succeeding in the assignments and exams. See our "Welcome" note and our philosophies of teaching and learning in ReggieNet.*

In this course, I like to connect the dots between theory and practice because they inform and rely on each other. Also, in the design of this course, I apply many of the practices and demands of the "real world" so you can become prepared for how you will be managed in your jobs. Lessons and skills in writing, critical thinking, and communication from other classes will be important.

Class Meetings

The following are policies about specific matters for class meetings.

- *Starting On Time*—The official starting time for class meetings is **not** your arrival time. Come early! We will begin on time, and this is why your assignments are due before/by the official starting time of class as stated in the semester schedule. Remember this and act on it: "Early is on time. On time is late. Late is unacceptable."
- *Finishing Early*—Whenever we finish our class meetings early, this still can be an important time for you to help your own learning at an individual level. Visit with me, talk with each other, or get things organized for yourself in that time. You may leave, if you wish. But remember that because we all have our class meetings already blocked off in our schedules, the time can be used well for your individual needs. And you can still visit with one of us during office hours and make appointments.
- *Continued/Open Topic Days*—A few days on the Course Schedule may be open-ended so that we can discuss subjects and issues that need extra time to cover or matters you want to cover not in the Course Schedule that are directly related to this course. For those days, you should submit ideas *a week or more in advance* so suitable preparation can be made for the class. Alternatively, if no ideas are offered, I will choose to address a topic that was raised in a prior class meeting that is worthy of more exploration. Anyone who submits ideas will be expected to play a lead role in class discussion, but I will assemble material for the class. Plan on being accountable for the material covered during these days on exams and assignments.

(Continued)

- *Late Start to Class*—On the very rare possibility that I am not in class promptly at the official starting time (or early), rest assured that I am on my way. Please remain in the classroom until I arrive. I will take attendance. We'll cover what material we can that is scheduled for that day. Any homework that is due will be collected. Any exam scheduled for that day will be given as planned.
- *Class Cancellation*—Only two conditions are likely to exist when classes are cancelled: (1) ISU's president has closed the university for a weather-related or another reason, or (2) I am unable to make it to ISU because of an illness, jury duty, or another situation. Either way, if class is cancelled, you will receive an official notice by e-mail. If I must cancel class, a notice will be posted in the classroom and/or on the doorway. Any assignment due or exam scheduled for a day when class is cancelled will be due or done at the next class meeting. If classes are cancelled and no assignment or exam is scheduled, we will forego covering the material we planned for that day and continue with material scheduled for the next class period. Any questions about material planned for a cancelled class meeting can be handled by visiting with me in my offices, sending an e-mail, using ReggieNet chat, or answering questions at the next class meeting. In either situation, expect me to hold class online through ReggieNet during an announced day and time to cover planned material, and attendance will be optional.

Attendance

Much of the material is only available through lecture and discussion. So, I expect to see you on a regular basis, and attendance will be taken daily. *Students with "perfect" attendance (i.e., students who do not miss any class meetings and/or have excused absences) will earn 20 extra-credit points at the end of the semester.* For an absence to be considered "excused," you must inform me prior to class, if at all possible. Excused absences include participation in a university-sanctioned event, the death of a family member (see University Policy and Procedures 2.1.27 Student Bereavement Policy online), incapacitating illness, and natural disaster. Other absences (e.g., cold/flu, weddings, babies, car trouble, house/apartment problem, etc.) will be considered individually. For any absence to be excused, I require written verification. If your absence will be extensive, contact the Dean of Students.

(Continued)

Six or more unexcused absences will result in one full letter-grade reduction for your final grade for the course.

My main objective with my attendance policy is to inspire you to take responsibility for "reporting to work" and, if you cannot, take responsibility for telling me why and having documentation whenever possible. This objective and policy is based on industry practices. "Blowing off" class/work is bad behavior.

Absences because of personal/vacation travel I typically will not excuse because the university's academic calendar has been out and everyone should have used it when planning such travel so that it doesn't interfere with school. (This is equivalent to when companies don't let employees take vacations when business needs are too high.) I may grant exceptions when travel had to have been booked significantly in advance and there is documentation to that effect.

Late arrival to class (i.e., less than 30 minutes after class begins) will not be penalized under the attendance policy, although I may note you were late on the attendance sheet. Late arrival after 30 minutes of class qualifies as an unexcused absence. Remember to sign in! If an assignment is due and you are late, the penalty for late work will be enforced. (See "Assignments" section of the syllabus.) If you drive to campus, always give yourself time to find a parking spot and get to class—at least twice the amount of time you think you need. And that should be the rule whether you drive to campus from town or from some other area of the state or country.

If you miss class or are late, you are responsible for obtaining all assignments, notes, and any other information that is given in class. I will not "re-teach" material for you, although I'd be glad to answer specific questions. Again, excused absences and late arrivals (less than 30 minutes after class begins) will not count against you.

Online Communication

I use e-mail to communicate directly to you as an individual and as a class, which you can also access through My.IllinoisState.edu. Clean out and check your ISU e-mail account frequently for notes or announcements from me, your fellow students, the department, and the college. *Not checking your e-mail or ReggieNet is not grounds for any excuse for not doing or not doing well on any assignment. It's your responsibility to (1) keep your e-mail accounts open and up-to-date and (2) monitor your e-mail and ReggieNet class news frequently.*

(Continued)

You must get used to the fact that good language use is necessary in every written document you prepare. This includes e-mail. I will only open and respond to your e-mail to me within 24 hours when:

1. A clear and simple subject line is given that, within 10 words or less, says exactly which class you're in and what topic(s) you're writing about. Don't be lazy and leave an old subject line from a previous e-mail I sent that has nothing to do with your e-mail's content. I will not reply to e-mail that recycles old subject lines that are not directly related to your e-mail content.
2. Your e-mail text is written effectively and concisely, and it should be as free of errors as possible.

By the way, I will apply these rules when I send e-mail to you.

Online Course Material

I use ReggieNet extensively to organize the material for this course and make announcements about our class. You can access ReggieNet through your homepage after you sign in to My.IllinoisState.edu. If you have problems with ReggieNet, let me know *and* call the Help Desk at 309-438-4357.

The ReggieNet site for this class contains additional, required reading material for this course. This material used in connection with the course may be subject to copyright protection. Your viewing of the material posted on ReggieNet does not imply any right to reproduce, to retransmit, or to redisplay it other than for your own personal or educational use. Links to other sites are provided for the convenience of the site user (staff or student) or visitor and do not imply any affiliation or endorsement of the other site owner nor a guarantee of the quality or veracity of information contained on the linked site.

Many files are PDFs and should open easily with Adobe Acrobat Reader to view and print them. If you don't have this free software, go to http://www.adobe.com to download that software.

Academic Dishonesty

Plagiarism and any other form of academic dishonesty will not be tolerated. Plagiarism (presenting someone else's work as your own or without proper acknowledgment) or any other type of academic dishonesty will

(Continued)

be considered justification for failure for that particular assignment or the entire course, depending on severity. Although you may discuss with each other any assignment and course material, bounce ideas off each other, and share the university's resources available to you (e.g., media guides), you cannot share actual work you do with others. All work must be that of the student (or students involved in a group assignment) and developed during the current semester for this course. Sources must receive credit using APA style. For information regarding academic integrity and procedures for academic misconduct, see ISU's Code of Student Conduct, Section IV.A.1.

Assignments Feedback

I give my most focused comments on the first page or two of your papers because after that the errors/problems are repetitive. I may note other things in later pages, but a lack of comments is not necessarily an indication of correctness or effectiveness. I also won't find absolutely everything because time is of the essence, and getting you feedback sooner than later serves you and me well. I firmly believe that my detailed comments and corrections in the first page or two are enough to indicate to you what I see, and you should learn from and look for those things elsewhere in the paper. Of course, if you want more detailed help, visit with me.

Assignments Expectations

If you go into the field of public relations or other field of communication for a career, you will be paid to be your organization's best communicators in all forms—written and oral, physical and virtual, interpersonal and public. I designed this course around this premise, and I try to approximate "real-world" problems, pressures, and planning that you will need to both enter and succeed in PR. The assignments (except for exams) are designed with ambiguity built in, which should inspire you to think analytically about what you know and what you're learning. So, I expect you to have questions about the assignments because in the "real world" you do not get precise recipes for everything you need to do—you'll have a college degree, probably one or more internships, and a job where you'll be paid to figure things out, so build this skill set now. (See my philosophy of teaching and learning.)

(Continued)

All assignments are due no later than the official starting time for class on the dates indicated in the "Course Outline" section of the syllabus. Assignments received after the official starting time of class (even one second late) but before it is dismissed, will be considered late and will be penalized 50% of the earned points. Electronic copies of your completed assignments may be accepted through e-mail by the class' official starting time (as indicated by the e-mail's time stamp) ONLY if you will miss class or if you believe you will be late to class. If you will be late, you still must turn in the hard copy. Assignments received after the class session is dismissed may be evaluated but will not receive credit. You may choose to turn in work in advance of the due date—especially if you are going to be absent the day something is due. I will critique all work that is submitted; however, if a paper is not even remotely close to the assignment given in class, I reserve the right to withhold all points. Documentation supporting a excused absence or late arrival to class would be applied to forgive the penalty for late work. Also see the "Course Grading Policy" section in the syllabus.

Class discussion involves going beyond the assigned readings. Assignments and exams formally challenge students to make sense of ambiguous situations and develop creative, appropriate and effective communication solutions based on the course's content and additional research. Assessment of students' learning against the course's objectives shall be done through a combination of activities. (See the grading policy in the syllabus. Also see my philosophy of teaching and learning.)

The writing assignments in this course are meant to (1) apply principles and concepts covered in this course to realistic problems and (2) build upon and challenge you to improve your current skill level—to be more consistent with "real-world" demands. All written work is expected to fulfill the assignments' contexts, purposes, and audiences just as they would if they were to be written to meet actual client needs. (See other material about writing expectations provided for this class.) *If the writing in any assignment does not meet this expectation, I reserve the right to withhold any or all points, depending on the severity of the writing's inappropriateness/ineffectiveness.*

Good writing is *both* strong in content and technically correct in its presentation (i.e., grammar, style, discourse conventions, layout, and printing). All written work must fulfill the content requirements given in the assignments, conform to American Psychological Association (APA) and (where applicable) Associated Press (AP) styles, and be free of grammar, spelling, style, and English usage errors.

(Continued)

Assignments' scores will be posted on ReggieNet and discussed in class. See the course schedule for details about all coursework. Please visit with me if you have any questions about any assignment or if you'd like me to give you some feedback about your work in progress. Score sheets for specific assignments are found in the "Assignments" area of the course's ReggieNet site. You'll need to print out the score sheet designed for each assignment and submit it with your assignment. *If you turn in an assignment without a score sheet, five (5) points will be automatically deducted from the total earned points for the assignment.*

If an assignment is missed for a reason deemed satisfactory by me, the same or a make up assignment of observably greater difficulty may be required. Documentation for absences or late arrivals on days when assignments are due will also be required.

For your own protection, you are expected to keep disk copies and/or photocopies of all assignments submitted to me. As you work on any computer remember to save your work frequently, always backup your work on another disk or other medium, and always protect your files and computer from viruses. *I will not accept work turned in late because you had technology problems and did not follow these cardinal rules for technology use or couldn't find a computer to use.*

"Prewriting"

The first draft of any public relations or advertising writing is seldom successful. Most writing goes through numerous drafts until the writer and the client are satisfied. In this class, we do not have the time to simulate this experience; thus, we will not rewrite assignments for credit. Instead of rewrites, I encourage you to engage in "prewrites." By this I mean you prepare draft material in advance of the deadlines and visit with one of us to review your work "in progress" and ask questions. This way you get feedback on the basic content and style of your writing—to see if you are on "the right track." *Note that prewrites are not "pregrading": I will not look for everything that is good/bad or right/wrong, but I will point out aspects or patterns of your writing that work or are problematic. I also will not do proofreading—that is your job.* Time permitting, prewrites can take place during class, but it's usually best during our office hours or appointments. E-mail prewrites are only granted in extreme situations. *Only two prewrites are allowed per assignment.*

(Continued)

Returned Work

I will make every effort to return work to you promptly. Most short assignments will be returned at the next class. Longer assignments may take one or two weeks. I will only return assignments to their authors. If you are not in class when an assignment is returned, please pick it up during your respective professor's office hours.

Keep Your Work for Job Hunting

If you plan to pursue a career in public relations or other field, having a set of solid examples of your work in a "professional portfolio" will be important for you to get an internship and/or your first full-time job. So make sure you keep very clean copies of the work you do in this and all your PR classes. Remember: no matter what score you received on any assignment, look for ways to make your examples even better, if not "perfect." Outside of your coursework, you may ask for some help from us in the PR faculty while you make your portfolio.

NOTE: We may alter aspects of these policies and the syllabus as the course progresses. You are responsible for noting any such changes, which will be announced in class and/or posted on ReggieNet.

ASSESSMENT MANUAL FOR COM 373
INTERNAL PUBLIC RELATIONS
Peter M. Smudde, Ph. D., APR

TABLE OF CONTENTS

LEARNING OBJECTIVES FOR THE COURSE

1. Identify characteristics and practices of internal communications in organizations.
2. Recall and apply key concepts, terms and principles for the operations and management of internal communications functions.
3. Analyze effective communications functions and recognize "best practices."
4. Demonstrate command of the process and use of language by analyzing cases and solving specific communication problems.
5. Connect principles and practices about successful communications within this course, across other courses and students' experiences.
6. Prepare students for work in a professional setting in terms of how they will be expected to think and act when given internal communications challenges.
7. Nurture an attitude of and introduce resources for life-long learning about effective internal communications.

LEARNING ASSESSMENTS TYPES

Assessment of students' learning against the course's objectives shall be done through a combination of learning assessments, which are detailed in this document and shown in the course diagram. All the learning assessments for this course fall into the following two categories:

(Continued)

- Formal/Graded Assessments—I can measure how well you can apply your learning by evaluating the *work you produce* in response to specific assignments. This work is what is graded and used to determine your final, overall level of mastery of the course's material by course's end. Graded assessments are weekly time sheets, strategic plan project, two papers, portfolio, and exams. Specific requirements and expectations for each formal assessment shall be provided separately. Also see the "Course Policies" section in the syllabus for matters that pertain to assignments' requirements.
- Informal/Ungraded Assessments—I can measure how well you are learning *in process* by observing, listening to and talking with you. These data reveal your personal processes, attitudes, and other matters that are part of how and how well you learn. Examples include chatting about course material before and during class, the quality of questions and discussion in class, the amount of sharing/disclosure, learning ownership, assignment discussion, visits with me, and attitude.

FORMAL LEARNING ASSESSMENTS

The purpose of the **job description paper** is for students to investigate the requirements, expectations, and scope of executive-level jobs in the PR field.

By the end of the job description paper, students will understand what it takes to work as an iPR professional in a corporation or an agency.

To accomplish the purpose, students will use any job search resources and the readings for this topic to explain the kinds of credentials, experiences, and demands for executive-level/management positions.

We will know the purpose was accomplished when the students write a paper that (1) "connects the dots" between the career principles in advertising and PR and the practical job requirements and (2) upholds the expectations for academic writing in the assignment, syllabus, and elsewhere.

The purpose of the **research paper** is for students to examine the literature they find for ideas and approaches about the basic nature and scope of internal communications.

By the end of the project, students will be able to show a broad understanding of the iPR function—what it is, what it covers, what is its organizational role, and what value contributions it gives to organizations and their internal publics.

(Continued)

To accomplish the purpose, students will use a variety of journals, books, and other credible sources that cover the subject area and related subject areas.

We will know the purpose was accomplished when the students produce a focused, well-argued, thorough, and effective paper that adheres to the overall expectations for the assignment.

The purpose of the **discourse examples and analysis** assignment is to help students become familiar with the kinds of communication media iPR professionals may use.

Through assessment, students will use assigned readings and additional research to guide them when identifying, collecting, and analyzing examples.

To accomplish the purpose, students will collect at least five (**5**) actual, real-world, different, and individual examples of internal public relations discourse for use in class.

We will know the purpose was accomplished when the students' collections of examples are scored based on the assignment's criteria.

The purpose of the **iPR project** is for students to experience the full process for developing a strategic iPR plan for an organization, using a scenario based on a real case example.

By the end of the iPR project, students will be able to think strategically and prepare a strategic plan for internal public relations that is thorough, accurate, complete, and well-written.

To accomplish the purpose, students will develop the strategic plan systematically and on their own schedules leading up to the final due date, using skills in research, analytical thinking, problem solving, and writing.

We will know the purpose was accomplished when students produce a complete iPR strategic plan that fulfills the assignment's requirements.

The purpose of **exams, if given**, is to measure students' individual recall of and analytical thinking about concepts, principles, and applications.

By the end of each exam, students will know the degree to which they have a command of course concepts, principles, and applications.

To accomplish the purpose, students will apply their accumulated knowledge and lessons from class to take each exam in the format and timeframe scheduled.

We will know this purpose was accomplished when students perform well on an exam.

(Continued)

The purpose of **penalties** for high-tech violations is to inspire students to be mindful about the impact and courteous use of technology with others in the same space.

Through the presence and, if needed, enforcement of penalties, students will adopt good behaviors about their use of high-tech devices.

To accomplish the purpose, students will follow the "Class Policy" document.

We will know this purpose was accomplished when students do not have any high-tech penalties.

INFORMAL LEARNING ASSESSMENTS

The purpose of **learning growth** is for students to become aware of their role in the co-creation of the learning environment for all of us.

Through learning-growth behaviors, students will advance their own learning, contribute to each other's learning, and promote a positive atmosphere for learning.

To accomplish the purpose, students will embrace the challenges in the course and add value to the course's learning experience.

We will know the purpose was accomplished when the students converse energetically about class material, ask good questions about ideas in the course, share or disclose matters about their learning and the course, own their learning, discuss assignments well, visit with the professor, and uphold a good attitude.

The purpose of **class citizenship** is to, given the policies stated in the syllabus, inspire students to contribute well to the learning environment of the class at every class meeting.

By the end of the semester, students will be satisfied with participating in class and, especially, growing in their own and each other's learning about PR education.

To accomplish the purpose, students will demonstrate individual contributions to class discussion; professional, ethical and respectful communication behaviors; and class attendance.

We will know the purpose was accomplished when the students participate in the class in ways that fulfill the assignment's requirements according to the associated rubric.

(Continued)

The purpose of the **learning ownership** is to observe the degree to which students willingly accept responsibility for what and how they learn material in the course and about the field.

Through learning ownership, students will exhibit behaviors and attitudes that reflect personal accountability of their learning.

To accomplish the purpose, students will express their personal ownership of their learning by how they talk about their performance in the class.

We will know the purpose was accomplished when the students openly make statements about their personal views regarding what they have learned and their class performance.

The purpose of **attitude** is to observe how much students involve themselves in the course, specifically, and the field, generally.

Through attitude, students will demonstrate their commitment to the subject and its potential impact on their futures.

To accomplish the purpose, students will be involved in class meetings on various levels—personal, interpersonal, and social.

We will know the purpose was accomplished when the students come to class early or on time, are part of class discussions, exhibit friendliness to others, and express interest in additional learning opportunities.

The purpose of the **quality of questions about ideas in the course** is to observe students' intellectual wrestling with the course's material.

Through questions about ideas, students will demonstrate a high caliber of thinking about the course's material.

To accomplish the purpose, students will ask focused and thoughtful questions that connect the dots among concepts within and beyond the course.

We will know the purpose was accomplished when the students probe more deeply the material in the course through their questions and comments.

The purpose of **sharing and disclosures** is to observe students' willingness to freely express their innermost thoughts, concerns, musings, etc. about the course and their learning.

Through sharing and disclosures, students will contribute to the social fabric of the class and learning environment.

To accomplish the purpose, students will reveal personal comments (e.g., compliments, confessions, criticism) that pertain to the course, the field, and learning.

(Continued)

We will know the purpose was accomplished when the students voluntarily and courteously share/disclose matters on their minds that pertain to the course and their learning.

The purpose of any **reading assignment** about given topics on the course calendar is to prepare students with a core of common understanding about the subject matter to participate in the next class discussion.

By the end of each reading assignment, students will be able to understand key topics in each of the assigned readings.

To accomplish the purpose, students will bring one note card per topic with five critical points that support each topic to the next class and/ or solve one or more of any chapter's exercises.

We will know this purpose was accomplished when students use their note cards to make their arguments during in-class discussion.

The purpose of **note taking** is for students to develop skills in recording key information and thinking about readings and during class meetings that will help them learn and apply concepts to in-class discussions, assignments, and exams.

By the end of each class meeting, students will have created a usable record of information and thinking that builds on prior meetings, connects dots with readings, and functions as a touchstone for future work.

To accomplish the purpose, students will pay attention in class, write key information and thinking in a medium that works for them, ask questions to clarify things, and be ready to apply their notes to class.

We will know this purpose was accomplished when students actively seek ways to ensure their notes are up-to-date, complete, organized, and used, including during meetings with the professor.

The purpose of **chatting before and during class** is to observe students' active discussion about course material.

Through buzzing, students will find ways each other understands and applies course material.

To accomplish the purpose, students will talk about course material voluntarily or in response to a prompt about a day's topic.

We will know the purpose was accomplished when the students' conversations about course material are energetic and on topic.

The purpose of **assignment comments/inquiries** is to observe students' critical analysis of expectations and parameters for

(Continued)

assignments, including, if appropriate, the consideration of revisions to improve an assignment.

Through assignment comments/inquiries, students will show their interest in the work they are to do and how it fits into the course's big picture.

To accomplish the purpose, students will think and ask questions about assignments.

We will know the purpose was accomplished when the students' comments/inquiries have yielded sufficient discussion, clarity, and, perhaps, improvements in an assignment.

The purpose of **lectures** is to organize and clarify complex ideas from assigned readings for students.

By the end of each lecture, students will be able to articulate positions on a given day's topic, connecting dots between what they know and what they are coming to know.

To accomplish the purpose, students will have read assigned readings, ask questions, share observations, and otherwise demonstrate engagement with a given day's topic.

We will know this purpose was accomplished when students accurately and appropriately use ideas, terms, principles, etc. in their in-class and assigned work.

The purpose of **individual work in class** is for students to make sense of material according to a particular prompt about the day's topic.

By the end of individual work, students will identify specific matters that are clear/unclear, complete/incomplete, or relevant/irrelevant to the day's topic and/or the course.

To accomplish the purpose, students will follow specific directions that direct their attention to the day's topic and some application of it to a real-world matter of PR management.

We will know this purpose was accomplished when students experience an "aha moment."

The purpose of any **collaborative learning technique (CoLT)** about given topics on the course calendar is to allow students to play with the concepts being covered during a given class meeting.

By the end of each CoLT, students will be able to connect the dots between concepts and their application to a specific aspect of the management of public relations.

(Continued)

To accomplish the purpose, students must have completed assigned readings and follow specific directions for the CoLT to solve a particular problem and explain the solution to the class.

We will know this purpose was accomplished when students develop a sound solution to the problem they tackled in the CoLT.

The purpose of **professor visits** is for students to obtain additional guidance in their processes for completing work and understanding material in the course.

Through professor visits, students will engage in focused conversation with the professor about the matters that matter most to them.

To accomplish the purpose, students will have a clear agenda of topics they want to address and, if necessary, be willing to deviate from that agenda into other areas that help their learning.

We will know the purpose was accomplished when the students visit with the professor and the visit was engaging and productive.

The purpose of **studying for exams** is to clarify and solidify material in students' minds.

By the end of studying for exams, students will be able to any answer question related to course material.

To accomplish the purpose, students will take advantage of a study guide, their notes, readings, instructor conferences, each other, and other course material. A study guide functions as a way to organize material covered in the course up to the point in the semester when an exam is given.

We will know this purpose was accomplished when students perform well on an exam.

The purpose of **in-class exam reviews** is for students to be prepared to effectively and efficiently take the exam.

By the end of an in-class review, students will understand the design and demands of the exam.

To accomplish the purpose, students will ask questions about material on which they want clarification and work out example questions, perhaps directly from the exam.

We will know the purpose was accomplished when students perform well on the exam.

The purpose of **communication** is for students to practice and improve skills in speaking and writing with each other and the professor because communication is the students' profession in PR.

(Continued)

Through each communication opportunity, ranging from formal assignments, to e-mail, to casual conversations, students will gain heightened awareness about what they do in their speaking and writing and how well they do it.

To accomplish the purpose, students will pay attention to themselves and improve their habits of expression in oral and written discourse that is formal and informal alike.

We will know the purpose was accomplished when the students (1) catch themselves making or on the verge of making mistakes and correcting them and (2) consistently communicate well in all respects, especially for formal, graded work.

COURSE DIAGRAM

The transformational goal for the course is a statement about how students should change as a result of their learning in this course about internal public relations. The categories of study in the ovals organize how the various learning assessments are applied to student learning. Notice how any assessment can be applied to contribute learning in the contexts of multiple categories and, thereby, contribute to achieving the course's transformational goal. The application of the learning assessments in each area of study is summarized in the sections that follow.

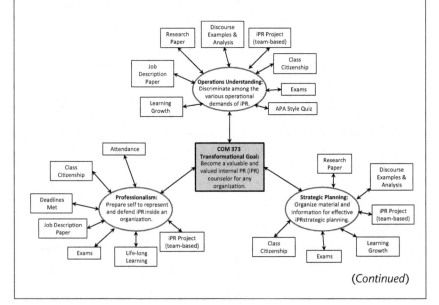

(Continued)

OPERATIONS UNDERSTANDING

The purpose of the **job description paper** is for students to investigate the requirements, expectations, and scope of executive-level jobs in the PR field.

By the end of the job description paper, students will understand what it takes to work as an iPR professional in a corporation or an agency.

To accomplish the purpose, students will use any job search resources and the readings for this topic to explain the kinds of credentials, experiences, and demands for executive-level/management positions.

We will know the purpose was accomplished when the students write a paper that (1) "connects the dots" between the career principles in advertising and PR and the practical job requirements and (2) upholds the expectations for academic writing in the assignment, syllabus, and elsewhere.

The purpose of the **research paper** is for students to examine the literature they find for ideas and approaches about the basic nature and scope of internal communications.

By the end of the project, students will be able to show a broad understanding of the iPR function—what it is, what it covers, what is its organizational role, and what value contributions it gives to organizations and their internal publics.

To accomplish the purpose, students will use a variety of journals, books, and other credible sources that cover the subject area and related subject areas.

We will know the purpose was accomplished when the students produce a focused, well-argued, thorough, and effective paper that adheres to the overall expectations for the assignment.

The purpose of the **discourse examples and analysis** assignment is to help students become familiar with the kinds of communication media iPR professionals may use.

Through assessment, students will use assigned readings and additional research to guide them when identifying, collecting, and analyzing examples.

To accomplish the purpose, students will collect at least five (**5**) actual, real-world, different, and individual examples of internal public relations discourse for use in class.

We will know the purpose was accomplished when the students' collections of examples are scored based on the assignment's criteria.

(Continued)

The purpose of the **iPR project** is for students to experience the full process for developing a strategic iPR plan for an organization, using a scenario based on a real case example.

By the end of the iPR project, students will be able to think strategically and prepare a strategic plan for internal public relations that is thorough, accurate, complete, and well-written.

To accomplish the purpose, students will develop the strategic plan systematically and on their own schedules leading up to the final due date, using skills in research, analytical thinking, problem solving, and writing.

We will know the purpose was accomplished when students produce a complete iPR strategic plan that fulfills the assignment's requirements.

The purpose of **exams, if given**, is to measure students' individual recall of and analytical thinking about concepts, principles, and applications.

By the end of each exam, students will know the degree to which they have a command of course concepts, principles, and applications.

To accomplish the purpose, students will apply their accumulated knowledge and lessons from class to take each exam in the format and timeframe scheduled.

We will know this purpose was accomplished when students perform well on an exam.

The purpose of **APA style quiz** (in-class or take-home) is for students to demonstrate their understanding of how to use APA style.

By the end of the APA style quiz, students will know the degree to which they can accurately and effectively apply APA style rules.

To accomplish the purpose, students will use the APA manual to solve multiple realistic problems that concern selected requirements of APA style that dominate the course's assignments.

We will know the purpose was accomplished when students perform well on a quiz.

STRATEGIC PLANNING

The purpose of the **research paper** is for students to examine the literature they find for ideas and approaches about the basic nature and scope of internal communications.

By the end of the project, students will be able to show a broad understanding of the iPR function—what it is, what it covers, what is its

(Continued)

organizational role, and what value contributions it gives to organizations and their internal publics.

To accomplish the purpose, students will use a variety of journals, books, and other credible sources that cover the subject area and related subject areas.

We will know the purpose was accomplished when the students produce a focused, well-argued, thorough, and effective paper that adheres to the overall expectations for the assignment.

The purpose of the **discourse examples and analysis** assignment is to help students become familiar with the kinds of communication media iPR professionals may use.

Through assessment, students will use assigned readings and additional research to guide them when identifying, collecting, and analyzing examples.

To accomplish the purpose, students will collect at least five (**5**) actual, real-world, different, and individual examples of internal public relations discourse for use in class.

We will know the purpose was accomplished when the students' collections of examples are scored based on the assignment's criteria.

The purpose of the **iPR project** is for students to experience the full process for developing a strategic iPR plan for an organization, using a scenario based on a real case example.

By the end of the iPR project, students will be able to think strategically and prepare a strategic plan for internal public relations that is thorough, accurate, complete, and well-written.

To accomplish the purpose, students will develop the strategic plan systematically and on their own schedules leading up to the final due date, using skills in research, analytical thinking, problem solving, and writing.

We will know the purpose was accomplished when students produce a complete iPR strategic plan that fulfills the assignment's requirements.

The purpose of **learning growth** is for students to become aware of their role in the co-creation of the learning environment for all of us.

Through learning-growth behaviors, students will advance their own learning, contribute to each other's learning, and promote a positive atmosphere for learning.

(Continued)

To accomplish the purpose, students will embrace the challenges in the course and add value to the course's learning experience.

We will know the purpose was accomplished when the students converse energetically about class material, ask good questions about ideas in the course, share or disclose matters about their learning and the course, own their learning, discuss assignments well, visit with the professor, and uphold a good attitude.

The purpose of **exams if given**, is to measure students' individual recall of and analytical thinking about concepts, principles, and applications.

By the end of each exam, students will know the degree to which they have a command of course concepts, principles and applications.

To accomplish the purpose, students will apply their accumulated knowledge and lessons from class to take each exam in the format and timeframe scheduled.

We will know this purpose was accomplished when students perform well on an exam.

PROFESSIONALISM

The purpose of **life-long learning** is to nurture an attitude of and introduce resources for life-long learning about effective leadership and management in advertising and public relations.

By the end of the semester, students will have become familiar with a wide range of resources and heightened interest that can help them continue their learning.

To accomplish the purpose, students will take advantage of the concepts, skills, and material from all course content.

We will know the purpose was accomplished when the students express the value of material and lessons from the course in their job searches and careers.

The purpose of **deadlines** is for students to respect and fulfill deadlines in tune with real-world demands.

By the end of the semester, students will have developed habits for making sure they complete their work early or on time, even to the second they are due.

To accomplish the purpose, students will turn in their finished work no later than the official starting time for class and not one second late.

(Continued)

We will know the purpose was accomplished when a student's final score for an assignment does not reflect the penalty of 50% deduction of earned points for turning in the assignment late.

The purpose of the **job description paper** is for students to investigate the requirements, expectations, and scope of executive-level jobs in the PR field.

By the end of the job description paper, students will understand what it takes to work as an iPR professional in a corporation or an agency.

To accomplish the purpose, students will use any job search resources and the readings for this topic to explain the kinds of credentials, experiences, and demands for executive-level/management positions.

We will know the purpose was accomplished when the students write a paper that (1) "connects the dots" between the career principles in advertising and PR and the practical job requirements and (2) upholds the expectations for academic writing in the assignment, syllabus, and elsewhere.

The purpose of the **iPR project** is for students to experience the full process for developing a strategic iPR plan for an organization, using a scenario based on a real case example.

By the end of the iPR project, students will be able to think strategically and prepare a strategic plan for internal public relations that is thorough, accurate, complete, and well-written.

To accomplish the purpose, students will develop the strategic plan systematically and on their own schedules leading up to the final due date, using skills in research, analytical thinking, problem solving, and writing.

We will know the purpose was accomplished when students produce a complete iPR strategic plan that fulfills the assignment's requirements.

The purpose of **exams** is to measure students' individual recall of and analytical thinking about concepts, principles, and applications.

By the end of each exam, students will know the degree to which they have a command of course concepts, principles, and applications.

(Continued)

To accomplish the purpose, students will apply their accumulated knowledge and lessons from class to take each exam in the format and timeframe scheduled.

We will know this purpose was accomplished when students perform well on an exam.

The purpose of **attendance** is to inspire students to take responsibility for "reporting to work" and, if they cannot attend a class meeting, take responsibility for telling me why and having documentation whenever possible.

Through assessment, students may be rewarded after the semester's end for "perfect" attendance (i.e., no absences that are unexcused).

To accomplish the purpose, students will attend class on a regular basis and not be late, but if they must miss class, they must follow the attendance policy in the syllabus.

We will know the purpose was accomplished when the students with "perfect" attendance (i.e., students who do not miss any class meetings and/or have excused absences) earn 20 extra-credit points at the end of the semester.

COM 373

iPR Project ~ 200 points

You will work in small teams (3–4 people) on an internal public relations project. The project will entail research and problem-solving analysis that will lead to the formulation of a sound iPR solution, featuring "real-world" business writing components. The scenario, task description, and score sheet is below.

The Scenario (based on a real case)

Harte & Stanwicke International (HSI) is a market leader in providing fastening systems to aerospace, automotive, rail, and other industrial customers. HSI has five U.S. manufacturing facilities in Arizona, California, Connecticut, New York, and Texas, with approximately 1,500 employees. Following the trend of many employers today, HSI does not offer a defined benefit retirement program. Instead, HSI wants employees to share the responsibility of building a retirement savings. So, while participation in HSI's 401(k) plan was relatively good (66.4%), the company wanted to increase that number and help employees who weren't participating start saving through the plan. The company also wanted to encourage employees who already were participating to save more through the plan and to further understand the differences among the plan's investment funds. These objectives triggered a need for a targeted communication program that would capture employees' attention, increase the plan's perceived value, heighten employees' plan knowledge, and motivate them to enroll.

The audience for the communication campaign included all 1,470 employees eligible to participate in the 401(k) plan. HSI's workforce is very diverse and includes a large number of Hispanic, Puerto Rican, and Filipino employees, many of whom are not fluent in English. Only 30% of HSI's employee population has a college education. The remaining 70% hold blue-collar jobs in HSI's various manufacturing facilities. Given these demographics, HSI needs communication material in both English and Spanish, and must be inviting to read and easy to understand.

The project's specific objectives are to:

- Increase plan participation to 75% from 66.4%.
- Get at least 20% of existing participants to increase their contribution rate.

(*Continued*)

- Provide investment education to help employees understand their choices and diversify their money appropriately.
- Provide communication materials that were informative, interesting, easy to understand, and had a tie-in to the company's business.
- Gain at least 80% attendance of all employees at any meetings.

Your Task

Your team handles employee relations for HSI and is responsible for all iPR programs. One of you is the team leader, and all of you report to the Nancy Munn, vice president of marketing and communications. She wants you to design an iPR program for this opportunity and submit it to her in the form of a well-written **memo**. (Letterhead will be provided for you to use.) Use 12-point, business-like font for your memo. Use single spacing for the text.

In your memo, Munn also needs you to propose a thorough plan to achieve results within eight months so everything can be ready for the employee benefit sign-up period in November. The purpose of your memo is to give Munn what she needs to convince senior management what must be done to meet the objectives listed above. The following are the topics you *must* address:

- Very brief statement about the problem/opportunity, including risks and benefits
- Analysis about HSI employees that is essential in planning (i.e., state and interpret the stats)
- Research about best practices in benefits communication that matter to HSI's case (e.g., management, tactics, measurement, etc.)
- Key message platform (audience-centered)
- Possible strategies and tactics tied to the stated program objectives (e.g., use a table)
- Timing, budget and evaluation based on best practices (analysis of each is needed)
- Argument about the value this iPR effort will provide HSI over the short and long terms

COM 373 INTERNAL PUBLIC RELATIONS

iPR Project Score Sheet

Team Members' Names: _____

_____

Criteria	Rating Poor — Great	Weighting factor	Final score
The problem/opportunity, including risks and benefits, is concise and sufficient.	1 2 3 4 5 6 7 8 9 10	2.0	
Research is given about HSI employees that will help in planning.	1 2 3 4 5 6 7 8 9 10	2.0	
Research about best practices in benefits communication is given concisely and concretely that matters to HSI's case.	1 2 3 4 5 6 7 8 9 10	2.0	
Audience-centered key message platform is given and fits context.	1 2 3 4 5 6 7 8 9 10	2.0	
Objectives, strategies and tactics are shown together clearly and simply. Strategies are linked specifically to one or more objective. Tactics are associated with each strategy and make sense within the context of the associated objective(s).	1 2 3 4 5 6 7 8 9 10	2.0	
Timing of the project is defined reasonably and specifically, including analysis of the program in context.	1 2 3 4 5 6 7 8 9 10	2.0	
Budget for the project is clear, reasonably detailed, and sufficiently analyzed to understand resource allocations.	1 2 3 4 5 6 7 8 9 10	2.0	
Evaluation method is summarized, tied to the stated objectives, reasonable, and anchored in best practices.	1 2 3 4 5 6 7 8 9 10	2.0	
The sort- and long-term value to HSI is argued well, using good evidence and sound reasoning.	1 2 3 4 5 6 7 8 9 10	2.0	

(Continued)

Criteria	Rating		Weighting factor	Final score
	Poor	Great		
The writing and presentation/format of the assignment is effective in its technical use of language, organization of content, and the visual presentation of the content.	1 2 3 4 5 6 7 8 9 10		2.0	

See comments on the paper for details that pertain to the above evaluation criteria.

Subtotal Score: _____

Out of 200

Less Deductions (see syllabus): _____

TOTAL SCORE: _____

APPENDIX C: SUGGESTIONS FOR CURRICULAR AND EXTRACURRICULAR TEACHING AND LEARNING

There are various and valuable out-of-class, extracurricular opportunities that can be tapped to extend student learning through hands-on experience in or relevant to PR. The following is a list of such opportunities to start your planning.

- Encourage students to seek and obtain multiple PR internships or jobs in organizations that serve in the fields that interest them.
- Advise a student-run organization focused on public relations (e.g., PRSSA or AWC).
- Direct or advise an agency that serves real clients for their PR and other communication needs. The work can be for pay or *pro bono*. The agency could be part of a student-run organization instead of a stand-alone group.
- Obtain a client for one or more assignments in a class, where the students' work targets a client's real need for real PR work that fits the class. Possible clients are local nonprofit organizations, local new/start-up businesses, on-campus student-focused organizations, and institutional operating units.
- Arrange tours of agency or non-agency public relations operations.
- Invite professionals to host job shadowing opportunities for students.
- Encourage students to attend local, regional, national, or international conferences that focus on or feature programs about public relations.
- Guide undergraduate and graduate students in independent research projects they initiate.
- Include undergraduate or graduate students as co-authors of your own scholarship.
- Encourage students to attend the meetings of local professional organizations' chapters (e.g., PRSA, IABC, or AWC).
- Invite students to participate in local chapters of professional organizations as organizational leaders (e.g., local PRSA, IABC, or AWC chapters).

APPENDIX D: HELPFUL RESOURCES

In addition to the references in the chapters, this appendix lists publications, organizations, online media, and other sources that can be used to further investigate the material in this book.

Teaching and Learning

Bransford, J., Brown, A. L., & Cocking, R. R. (Eds.) (2000). *How people learn: Brain, mind, experience, and school* (expanded ed.). Washington, DC: National Academies Press.

Brown, A., & Green, T. D. (2006). *The essentials of instructional design: Connecting fundamental principles with process and practice.* Upper Saddle River, NJ: Pearson.

Brown, P. C., Roediger III, H. L., & McDaniel, M. A. (2014). *Make it stick: The science of successful learning.* Cambridge, MA: The Belknap Press of Harvard University Press.

Clark, R., Nguyen, F., & Sweller, J. (2006). *Efficiency in learning: Evidence-based guidelines to manage cognitive load.* San Francisco, CA: Pfeiffer, Wiley.

Dewey, J. (1997). *Experience and education.* New York: Free Press. (Original published 1938)

Douglas, A. (2000). Learning as participation in social practices: Interpreting, student perspectives on learning. *College English, 7,* 153–165.

Finkel, D. L. (2000). *Teaching with your mouth shut.* Portsmouth, NH: Boynton/Cook.

Henson, K. T. (2003). Foundation for learner-centered education: A knowledge base. *Education, 124*(1), 5–16.

Jensen, E. (2005). *Teaching with the brain in mind* (2nd ed.). Alexandria, VA: Association for Supervision and Curriculum Development.

Jonassen, D. H., & Hernandez-Serrano, J. (2002). Case-based reasoning and instructional design: Using stories to support problem solving. *Educational Technology Research and Development, 50,* 65–77.

Kuh, G. D., Kinzie, J., Schuh, J. H., & Whitt, E. J. (2005). *Student success in college: Creating conditions that matter.* San Francisco, CA: Jossey-Bass.

Reiser, R. A. (2001). A history of instructional design and technology: Part II: A history of instructional design. *Educational Technology Research and Development, 49*(2), 57–67.

Zull, J. E. (2002). *The art of changing the brain: Enriching the practice of teaching by exploring the biology of learning.* Sterling, VA: Stylus Publishing.

Scholarship of Teaching and Learning (SoTL)

Huber, M. T. (2004). *Balancing acts: The scholarship of teaching and learning in academic careers.* Sterling, VA: Stylus.

Huber, M. T., & Morreale, S. P. (Eds.) (2002). *Disciplinary styles in the scholarship of teaching and learning: Exploring common ground.* Sterling, VA: Stylus.

Hutchings, P. (Ed.) (2000). *Opening lines: Approaches to the scholarship of teaching & learning.* Menlo Park, CA: The Carnegie Foundation for the Advancement of Teaching.

McKinney, K. (2007). *Enhancing learning through the scholarship of teaching and learning: The challenges and joys of juggling.* San Francisco, CA: Anker.

McKinney, K. (Ed.) (2013). *The scholarship of teaching and learning in and across the disciplines.* Bloomington, IN: Indiana University Press.

Weimer, M. (2006). *Enhancing scholarly work on teaching and learning: Professional literature that makes a difference.* San Francisco, CA: Jossey-Bass.

Werder, C., & Otis, M. M. (Eds.) (2010). *Engaging student voices in the study of teaching and learning.* Sterling, VA: Stylus Publishing.

Publishing

Boice, R. (1990). *Professors as writers: A self-help guide to productive writing.* Stillwater, OK: New Forums Press.

Booth, W. C., Colomb, G. G., & Williams, J. M. (2008). *The craft of research* (3rd ed.). Chicago, IL: University of Chicago Press.

Boyer, E. L. (1997). *Scholarship reconsidered: Priorities of the professoriate.* San Francisco, CA: Jossey-Bass.

Fyffe, R., & Walter, S. (2005). Building a new future: Preparing "future faculty" and "responsible conduct of research" programs as a venue for scholarly communication discussions. *College & Research Libraries News, 66*(9), 654–663.

Germano, W. (2001). *Getting it published: A guide for scholars and anyone else serious about serious books.* Chicago, IL: University Press.

Glassick, C. E., Huber, M. T., & Maeroff, G. I. (1997). *Scholarship assessed: Evaluation of the professoriate.* San Francisco, CA: Jossey-Bass.

Huff, A. S. (1998). *Writing for scholarly publication.* Thousand Oaks, CA: Sage.

McDaniel, T. R. (2007). Rethinking scholarly publication for tenure. *Academic Leader, 23*(3), 8.

Sargent, C. F. (2006, November/December). Five persistent publishing myths among scholarly authors with big-bookstore dreams. *Change, 38*(6), 23–28.

Scurr, R. (2007, March 9). Academic publishers are struggling to publicise more accessible books, many of which never reach wider readership. *Times Higher Education Supplement,* 13.

Straus, L. G. (2006). Academic responsibility, professionalism, and scholarly publication in the age of high corporate profits. *Journal of Anthropological Research, 62*(4), 593–595.

Thompson, J. B. (2005). Survival strategies for academic publishing. *Publishing Research Quarterly, 21*(4), 3–10.

Thompson, J. B. (2005, June 17). Survival strategies for academic publishing. *Chronicle of Higher Education, 51*(41), B6–B9.

Thyer, B. A. (1994). *Successful publishing in scholarly journals.* Thousand Oaks, CA: Sage.

Life and Career

American Association of University Professors (2015). *Policy documents & reports* (11th ed.). Baltimore, MD: Johns Hopkins University Press.

American Council on Education, American Association of University Professors, & United Educators (2000). *Good practice in tenure evaluation: Advice for tenured faculty, department chairs, and academic administrators.* Washington, DC: American Council on Education. Retrieved from https://www.aaup.org/sites/default/files/files/Good%20Practice%20in%20Tenure%20Evaluation.pdf

Ruiz, D. M., & Ruiz, D. J. (2010). *The fifth agreement: A practical guide to self-mastery (Toltec wisdom).* San Rafael, CA: Amber-Allen.

Sheen, F. J. (1983). *On being human: Reflections on life and living.* New York, NY: Image Books.

APPENDIX E: EXAMPLE PUBLIC RELATIONS PROGRAM ASSESSMENT PLAN COMPONENTS

1.0   Contextual Background

This document is a "skeleton" of an assessment plan that may be used for a public relations (PR) program at a college or university. It was developed for a prominent Midwestern university's PR program that also is CEPR. *The text in this section and the sections that follow are only examples.* This document's content was developed using a combination of sources, including the university's own approach to program assessment, the PR program's own planning documents, research about PR education, and CEPR criteria. All of this document, therefore, is purely a model of what a program assessment plan could look like and cover. All material can and should be revised for your own program as needed.

2.0   Assessment Objectives

- Assess the program's effectiveness in preparing graduates for careers in PR and related fields.
- Assess the program's effectiveness in developing the knowledge, skills, and abilities expected of new PR professionals on a daily basis.
- Discover gaps in curriculum content based on current practice and future trends in the PR field (industry and academia).
- Garner guidance from alumni about opportunities for continuous improvement in the PR curriculum and associated opportunities, such as Public Relations Student Society of America (PRSSA) and professional experiences.

- Establish a better systematic means for measuring the program's effectiveness to fulfill CEPR accreditation standards 1, 4, and 5 (B-02 and E-02).

3.0 Vision for the Public Relations Program

Be recognized as a top PR program in the state and, potentially, the region and nation.

4.0 Mission for the Public Relations Program

Bridge theory and practice about PR for students in effective ways that enable their active learning and preparation for a career in PR.

5.0 Overall Goals for the Public Relations Program

A. Ground the undergraduate PR major in specialized knowledge and theories.
B. Emphasize specialized knowledge, skills, and abilities in particular areas, especially writing, research, critical analysis and decision-making, media production, business, and project management.

6.0 Objectives for Student Learning in the Public Relations Program (Conceptual Definitions for Curriculum Content)

Based on Dee Fink's "taxonomy for significant learning" from his book *Creating Significant Learning Experiences* (2013), the following learning objectives comprise the assessment framework for student learning in the PR program:

1. Foundational knowledge: . . .
2. Application: . . .
3. Integration: . . .
4. Human dimension: . . .
5. Caring: . . .
6. Learning how to learn: . . .

7.0 Assessment Map

The following table simply shows where the required courses in the PR program target its core learning objectives (see Section 6.0). This map also correlates with the content of Section 13.0 to show where and how assessment measurements align with the program's objective.

	Curriculum Objectives (Section 6.0)					
Required Courses & Operational Definitions for Each	Objective 1	Objective 2	Objective 3	Objective 4	Objective 5	Objective 6

8.0   Requirements in the Public Relations Major

The following courses are required for graduation with a bachelor's degree in PR. These courses are the focus of this assessment plan, as they are the core requirements for the degree. Certain elective courses are recommended for PR majors, not formally addressed in this assessment plan, and presented in Section 14.0. The following are the criteria for graduation from the PR program:

- Credit hours needed overall: . . .
- Required courses with prerequisite courses: . . .
- Elective courses credit hours: . . .
- Minimum senior hours needed: . . .
- Internship recommended or required: . . .
- Minor or second major is encouraged: . . .

Required Courses	Course Descriptions & Prerequisites from the Catalog

9.0   CEPR Accreditation Standards

The PR program officially became a CEPR program in September 2013 and was renewed in 2019. To maintain the accreditation, we must uphold expectations for content, rigor, and learning that are articulated in eight standards for CEPR, only one of which is directly concerned with assessing student learning.

Plus, we must undergo accreditation reviews every six years. For this assessment plan, we will incorporate the expectations for each of these accreditation standards for our program assessment, and the standards are measured for the reaccreditation process every six years. The standards are as follows:

- *Standard One: PR Curriculum*—The PR curriculum should be sufficient to prepare students adequately for career growth in the field. In accord with *Fast Forward*, the 2018 report of the Commission on Public Relations Education, it should be well-grounded in liberal arts, communication, and business disciplines. Available courses specific to PR should include principles, writing, research, campaigns/case studies, and experiential learning. Through academic advising, students should be fully aware of requirements, prerequisites, and opportunities in electives and/or minors. Students should be able to progress through the program in a timely manner.
- *Standard Two: PR Faculty (Full- and Part-time)*—Faculty dedicated partially or fully to the PR program and classes should have appropriate experience and/or credentials. They should be effective mentors and prepare their students well for a career in PR. If they are research faculty, their research should strengthen their ability to teach and mentor students effectively. Part-time faculty should be selected based on experience and ability to teach and mentor and be well supervised to ensure the consistent quality of PR courses. Full- and part-time faculty should be actively engaged in the field and with other professionals.
- *Standard Three: Resources, Equipment, and Facilities*—The PR program should have equitable access to unit budgetary and other resources, facilities, library resources, and computer and desktop publishing facilities. Technology should be current and comparable to that used in the field.
- *Standard Four: PR Students*—The quality of the students in the program and the recruitment efforts to draw outstanding students into PR are the foundations of a successful educational program. Students should also receive adequate career counseling.
- *Standard Five: Assessment*—Quality academic programs should have routine and systematic assessment built into the curriculum and the program. Assessment should determine whether or not the program is meeting its academic and professional objectives.
- *Standard Six: Professional Affiliations*—The involvement of alumni and other practicing professionals in mentoring students into the profession is strongly desired. The program should help students begin to cultivate the professional relationships they will need throughout their careers. The opportunity to network through the PRSSA and/or other professional organizations is essential to preparation for the professional practice of PR. Strongly recommended are organizations affiliated with the Global Alliance for Public Relations and Communication Management.

- *Standard Seven: Relationships with Total Unit and University*—To provide adequate PR education, the program must depend upon other programs and faculty within their units and across the university who teach general education, liberal arts, business, and communications. The perception and reputation of the PR program, its faculty, and its students are factors in the quality of teaching and mentoring that will occur outside the program. Receiving the resources necessary for good PR education depends partially on these factors.
- *Standard Eight: Diversity and Global Perspectives*—It is important that PR education prepare students to serve and work in a diverse society. Educators must emphasize the importance of diversity and the roles of minority groups in teaching students to understand, communicate with, and relate to a multicultural/global society.

10.0   Standard for Public Relations Education

The Commission on Public Relations Education, in research-based reports about PR education (particularly for this assessment plan *Fast Forward*), (a) identified specific areas of knowledge and skills that must be taught in PR programs, (b) specified a liberal arts framework for undergraduate curriculum, and (c) defined major content areas for any PR curriculum. Each of these three dimensions is central to maintaining the CEPR accreditation standards for PR programs in higher education (see Section 9.0), which we must uphold as an accredited program. The support of knowledge and skills, undergraduate curriculum design, and undergraduate course content in *required* courses is given here (based on each course's content schedule stated in their respective syllabus) as a reference point for possible measurements against the student-learning objectives in Section 6.0 and in tune with the CEPR accreditation standards in Section 9.0. (NOTE: **e** = elective courses may apply; see Section 14.0.)

Knowledge	Supporting Courses	Skills	Supporting Courses
Communication and persuasion concepts and strategies		Research methods and analysis	
Communication and PR theories		Management of information	
Relationships and relationship-building		Mastery of language in written and oral communication	
Societal trends		Problem-solving and negotiation	
Ethical issues		Management of communication	

(Continued)

(Continued)

Legal requirements and issues		Strategic planning	
Marketing and finance		Issues management	
PR history		Audience segmentation	
Uses of research and forecasting		Informative and persuasive writing	
Multicultural and global issues		Community, consumer, and employee relations and other practice areas	
The business case for diversity		Technological and visual literacy	
Various world social, political, economic, and historical frameworks		Managing people, programs, and resources	
Organizational change and development		Sensitive interpersonal communication	
Management concepts and theories		Critical listening skills	
		Fluency in a foreign language	
		Ethical decision-making	
		Participation in the professional PR community	
		Message production	
		Working with current issues	
		Environmental monitoring	
		Public speaking and presentation	
		Applying cross-cultural and cross-gender sensitivity	

Undergraduate Curriculum	*Support*	*Undergraduate Course Content*	*Supporting Courses*
Built on foundation of liberal arts, social science, business, and language courses	Yes or No	Theory, origin, principles, and professional practice of PR	
Intertwine principles of PR and management with business, behavioral science, technology, and other disciplines	Yes or No	PR law and ethics	

Master principles of etiquette and professionalism	Yes or No	PR research, measurement and performance evaluation	
Integrate global concepts of globalization, diversity, and multiculturalism, and fluency in languages other than English is desirable	Yes or No	PR planning and management	
Emphasize ethics and organizational transparency as key to establishing trust and acceptance among publics	Yes or No	PR writing and production	
Understand current technology and its use, but must develop skills that will enable them to adapt to rapid changes and advancements	Yes or No	PR action and implementation	
Learn solid research skills and the ability to interpret and use research in decision-making	Yes or No	Supervised work experience in PR	
Incorporate the internal audience into PR planning and communication.	Yes or No	Disciplines related to PR	
		Directed electives	See Section 14.0

11.0   Micro-level Assessments

Direct and indirect assessments of student learning at the *course* and *student* levels are necessary for measuring program effectiveness. There are various ways to apply assessments of student learning (in synch with the content of Section 10.0), with direct assessment being the most essential. These "micro-level assessments" at the course and student levels, as the tables in Section 13.0 show, would reveal the following *evidence*:

- Course objectives are met.
- Prerequisite knowledge, skills, and abilities (KSAs) are retained and applied from prior coursework.
- Foundational knowledge is covered and applied.
- Areas for continuous improvement are identified and addressed (strengths, weaknesses, recommendations).
- Assignments cultivate many/most KSAs that are necessary and sufficient for new professionals (see CEPR standards).

Data gathering for micro-level assessments would come from *direct assessments* of students' work—tangible evidence from students of what they have and have not learned. The use of rubrics would be instrumental in codifying the criteria on which students' work would be evaluated within the specific context of given assignments and within the broader context of an overall course. Faculty would need to retain copies of all rubrics for all students' assignments (i.e., digital copies preferred) so that data about student performance can be used to drill down into what works and what doesn't work in courses and the PR program by tracking performance over time, at least in terms of the above list of evidence and reference points in Section 10.0. Methods for direct assessment include tests and quizzes, comprehensive exams, oral exams, interviews, papers, projects, case analyses, performances, exhibitions, and portfolios.

Data gathering for micro-level assessments also would come from *indirect assessments* of student learning—"proxy signs" outside of course-based assignments that show students probably learned content, especially through the reference points in Section 10.0. Methods for indirect assessment include student and alumni surveys, interviews, focus groups, and reflective essays; feedback about interns' performance (also can serve as direct evidence when coupled with a specific performance rubric); program reputation and quality; selected items from faculty course evaluations; retention and graduation rates; job placements; career advancements; honors and awards; and anecdotal information from individuals related to the program in any way.

12.0   Stakeholders as Assessors

The following groups of stakeholders would serve as *assessors* of student learning through direct and indirect measures. The abbreviations given are those that will be used in Section 13.0, where they best apply.

- Students (S)
- Faculty (F)
- Class clients (C)
- Internship/field experience supervisors (I)
- Alumni (A)
- Employers (E)

13.0   Assessment Design

The table presented in this section (in six parts, one for each program objective) shows the core learning objectives for the required courses in the PR program (see Section 6.0) and summarizes the means by which they are *presently* measured (direct and indirect), when they are measured, whether they are developed or not, and who assesses them. Only the courses that are mapped to a given program learning objective (see Section 7.0) are listed under that objective in the following table.

Multiple assessment techniques are permissible (see Sections 10.0 and 11.0). Sampling of class students' performance on direct and indirect assessments is permissible when developed and appropriate, and those assessments are taken based on assignments' stated requirements/criteria and, if available, rubrics for those assignments. See Section 15.0 for ideas on how to improve this assessment design after the implementation of this plan.

It is important to note that, although an internship is not required and, therefore, not in the following table, that course provides measurements (mainly direct, written assessments from supervisors) about student learning that support all seven of the program's learning objectives.

Learning Objectives (see Section 6.0)	Assessment Methods for Evidence of Student Learning Per Required Course (see Sections 10.0 and 11.0)		Timing	Developed/ Undeveloped	Assessors (see Section 12.0)
1.	Direct				
	Indirect:				

Learning Objectives (see Section 6.0)	Assessment Methods for Evidence of Student Learning Per Required Course (see Sections 10.0 and 11.0)		Timing	Developed/ Undeveloped	Assessors (see Section 12.0)
2.	Direct				
	Indirect:				

Learning Objectives (see Section 6.0)	Assessment Methods for Evidence of Student Learning Per Required Course (see Sections 10.0 and 11.0)		Timing	Developed/ Undeveloped	Assessors (see Section 12.0)
3.	Direct				
	Indirect:				

Learning Objectives (see Section 6.0)	Assessment Methods for Evidence of Student Learning Per Required Course (see Sections 10.0 and 11.0)		Timing	Developed/ Undeveloped	Assessors (see Section 12.0)
4.	Direct				
	Indirect:				

Learning Objectives (see Section 6.0)	Assessment Methods for Evidence of Student Learning Per Required Course (see Sections 10.0 and 11.0)		Timing	Developed/ Undeveloped	Assessors (see Section 12.0)
5.	Direct				
	Indirect:				

Learning Objectives (see Section 6.0)	Assessment Methods for Evidence of Student Learning Per Required Course (see Sections 10.0 and 11.0)		Timing	Developed/ Undeveloped	Assessors (see Section 12.0)
6.	Direct				
	Indirect:				

14.0 Recommended Elective Courses for the PR Major

The following courses are those in which students may enroll to fulfill their graduation requirements in the PR major. This list is presented here to complete the picture of the range of PR and PR-related courses students may take as PR majors. Students may, of course, elect to enroll in almost any course to fulfill their graduation requirements. Because these courses are not required in the PR major, they are not formally addressed in this assessment plan.

Recommended Elective Courses	Course Descriptions & Prerequisites from the Catalog

15.0 Options for Continuous Improvement

This assessment plan is flexible, so improvements can be made in areas that need them. The following list presents ideas we have for making this plan better over the course of its use. Some items may be accomplished sooner than others, and such improvements will depend on the complexity of their application and resource availability, especially time.

- Idea . . .
- Idea . . .
- Idea . . .
- Idea . . .

INDEX

Note: Page numbers in *italic* and **bold** refer to figures and tables, respectively.

Printed in the United States
by Baker & Taylor Publisher Services